For Deborah Rogers, with love and gratitude

Acknowledgements

I should like to express my gratitude to Jeremy Trevathan for suggesting that I write about Circe. I also wish to thank Jane Gregory for her stimulating company in the park, and Michael Gordon, the vet who cared for Circe throughout her life. My salutations to the ever-patient Tony Lacey and to the incomparable Zelda Turner.

Contents

Contents

After-Life

Early one evening in September 1990, I picked up the telephone and dialled a familiar number. The time was five past six. A couple of minutes later, I realized why I was getting no response. The friend I was calling had been dead since March.

I put down the phone and sat in silence for a while. My action had been happily automatic, I understood with dismay. I had forgotten, in my eagerness to communicate with her, that her sufferings were over and that she was lying in the same grave as the man she loved, in a quiet country churchyard. She was at rest and I, it seemed, was the perturbed spirit.

I had been living alone since the death of my long-term companion in 1986. Except that I wasn't on my own, in reality, because I had a dog for company. I had acquired her the previous year, in peculiar circumstances that are related in this collection of memories and musings. She enslaved me from the very first moment of seeing her, and as the months went by I began to wonder if I was starting to emulate J. R. Ackerley, that famous late convert to canine charm. I remembered that the poet William Plomer, a close friend of Ackerley and E. M. Forster, had told me how 'that bloody dog' had taken possession of Joe to such an extent that he and Forster were loath to visit the flat in Putney Ackerley shared with his adored Queenie. (Queenie is 'Evie' in the novel *We Think the World of You*, and 'Tulip' in the memoir *My Dog Tulip* – the curious little gems he wrote towards the end of his life.) Would my own friends and acquaintances hesitate before coming to see me for fear of being nipped and barked at by the tireless Circe? I hoped not, though some of them found the business of diverting her a bore, and occasionally said so.

But Circe was not like Queenie in any respect other than beauty. Joe had recognized a kindred, wounded spirit in the bitch he rescued from his lover's unthinking, working-class parents, whose idea of exercise was to let the creature out in the back yard, which was the size of the proverbial postage stamp. (Some neighbours of mine, the Patels, emigrants from Idi Amin's Uganda, kept an Alsatian to protect their newspaper and tobacco shop. They had been advised that an unexercised dog would be more ferocious at warding off intruders and burglars than a healthy, contented one. The unnaturally obese animal escaped when the Patels' children forgot to close the door behind the counter. The dog, sensing freedom, leapt over the display of sweets and chocolate bars, and dashed out of the shop. He must have run for miles, because he was never traced in west London.) Ackerley, like me, had been indifferent to dogs for most of his life. But the sight of the disconsolate, whimpering Queenie, and the feelings of outrage and pity it invoked, was to afford him an inseparable, loving relationship of a kind he had been unable to sustain with a succession of 'ideal' youths. Their relationship was so close, in fact, that Queenie's jealousy of Joe's friends became uncontainable.

Circe had known neither cruelty nor negligence when I chanced upon her in 1985. I had no cause to rescue her. It was clear from the outset that she would not be jealous of the people I knew, whom she invariably greeted with a welcoming bark and a briskly wagging tail. She was a flirt until the end of her days, never happier than when a gentle hand was stroking her tummy. Bitches have an embarrassing habit of attaching themselves to human legs in ways that appear sexually provocative, and Circe was just such a bitch. She showed a certain discrimination in her choice of leg, however, giving me reason to wonder why X's was preferable to Y's. Her chosen victim would laugh nervously, or blush from the shock of her abandoned advances, or call her a shameless tart while attempting to extricate himself from her passionate clutch.

Strangers, beguiled by the dog at my side, stopped to talk to her and, sometimes, to me. The strangest of these lonely, garrulous folk was Marjorie, who lived nearby with a bedraggled black mongrel, ignored by Circe, and a changing selection of cats. I could never quite place her accent, with its faint hint of Eastern Europe. Marjorie's chatter was concerned with the injustices meted out to the likes of us by Those in Authority. As she grew angrier, she tossed her head back and I was granted a view of her snarling, discoloured teeth.

Animals, bless them, were better than human beings, she maintained, and much more trustworthy. I nodded agreement.

Following the death of my companion, David, Marjorie felt compelled to offer me sympathy and commiseration. Except that she had our names confused, in spite of my quiet and firm efforts to correct her. 'You must be missing Paul, David,' she'd say, and I would respond 'I'm Paul. It's David who's dead.' Our meetings turned into a tiny comedy for me, thanks to her inevitable 'Paul's in heaven, bless him' and 'Paul's happier out of it' and 'You look happy today, David, like the cat who's got the cream' and an uncountable number of similar remarks.

She continued to address me as David, and I gave up insisting on my identity. Five years after the real David's death, I wrote a poem about my dual existence. I gave it the title 'After-Life':

Marjorie thinks I'm you, not me.
She calls me by your name. I've stopped
Correcting her. Some might say
I've given up the ghost.

Marjorie knows that one of us is dead.
She asks how long it is since I passed on.
'Five years,' I answer. She tells me I'm
At rest now, with the saints and angels.

Marjorie dotes on animals. She believes
They're silent witnesses for God, spying
On our behaviour. Their once-dumb tongues
Speak in that heaven I've gone to.

Marjorie's mad. Marjorie smells. Marjorie's
Best avoided. I only meet her when
I'm turning corners. Then I hear
You're looking well, considering; and young.

Marjorie moved out of the district, though she appears
occasionally – dogless now – to do a little shopping and chat
to old acquaintances. She walks with a stick, and is shabbier
than ever, her hair like an unruly bird's nest. I was on my way
to Hammersmith Hospital on a November afternoon in 2002
when I saw a familiar figure in a tatty overcoat shuffling
towards me. 'Hullo, David,' I heard. I was not myself again,
for the first time in ages. I told her where I was heading, and
that I had to keep an appointment with the chief cardiologist.
She suddenly clutched my arm with her free hand. 'Don't go
there,' she advised. 'They'll murder you in there, like they
tried to murder me. I wouldn't go there, David. Be very
careful. I want to die when God sees fit, not when they do.'

I freed myself from her grip, insisting that I didn't want to
be late.

'Take my advice, David. Be careful. Your heart belongs to
you, not them.'

'After-Life' was published in *The Times Literary Supplement*
in September 1991. Some weeks later, in Rome, I was flicking
through *La Repubblica* when I noticed my name and two lines
from the poem. The author of the piece seemed to think that
I'm a devout Roman Catholic and a devotee of St Francis of
Assisi. Marjorie's belief that animals are 'silent witnesses for
God, spying/ On our behaviour' was now attributed to me. I
was Paul, to be sure, but I was also Marjorie, the scruffy mystic.

*

Thanks to Circe, I made the acquaintance of Jane Gregory and her dog, a pretty piebald mongrel named Liquorice. She and Liquorice became best friends, but they occasionally fell out with each other, as best friends do. It was wonderful to watch Liquorice bounding across the grass to greet her, and delightful to see them swimming together in the small pond in the Conservation Area of Ravenscourt Park. They would flop into the sometimes stagnant water when the heat was too much for them, emerging sodden and dripping. Jane and I backed away as they vigorously shook themselves dry.

Jane is a successful literary agent, who represents the kind of authors I seldom read. She is red-haired, and of a fiery disposition. I trembled with fear on those occasions when she marched over to a brutish-looking individual with a large Alsatian or a Staffordshire bull terrier, trumpeting 'I have a spare bag if you need it.' The dog was invariably shitting on the open grass, where children played and grown-ups sunbathed. The offender would often accept the bag Jane was holding out to him with varying degrees of reluctant or embarrassed gratitude. She waited until he had picked up the turds, pointing to those he had missed or overlooked. 'That's better, isn't it?' she'd say when the spot was relatively clean again. 'Don't forget to bring your own bags next time.'

There was one spring day, not to be forgotten, when the sky turned green for a few moments. We looked up to see a flock of parakeets, and wondered if we were experiencing an optical illusion of a particularly unusual kind. But no, they were definitely parakeets, as their squawking reminded us. Where had they come from? Not far, probably. I learned in due course that a pair of these exotic creatures, male and female, had flown out of captivity as long ago as the 1920s.

They had built their nest in the grounds of Chiswick House, the exquisite folly modelled on Palladio's Villa Rotonda at Vicenza by the third Earl of Burlington between 1725 and 1729. Alexander Pope, Jonathan Swift, John Gay and Handel were among its earliest visitors. The discriminating birds had chosen this beautiful setting in which to breed. Their descendants must have migrated during the cold, foggy London winters, since it's impossible to imagine them surviving otherwise. Anyway, there they were, en route to Chiswick, perhaps – a free, happy, voluble family.

It was in a restaurant in a small town in Wiltshire that Jane Grigson introduced me to Jeremy Round, the first food writer and restaurant critic for the then fledgling newspaper, the *Independent*. I liked him instantly, because he talked as he wrote – with wit and verve and a sense of mischief. I was amused, as were many others, by the aptness of his name. His girth was Falstaffian, and became even more so during our sadly brief friendship. He addressed me as 'Doll' on that first encounter, and 'Doll' I remained.

He came to my flat with his partner – another Jeremy, whom he had met when they were students at Hull University. The two Jeremys were disconcerted to find out on arrival that I shared my life with an energetic dog. She welcomed them with a frenzy of barking. I had to assure them that the deafening racket was her way of demonstrating that they were acceptable to her – as, indeed, was true. Jeremy Trevathan was happier to be a sock-thrower than was Jeremy Round, who quickly tired of the game.

At the time, I was writing a monthly restaurant column for the *Daily Telegraph*, and the three of us often ate at the same places. I recall a Sunday spent in Worcester, where we dined in a newly opened bistro, staffed by enthusiastic teenagers. The boy who waited on us was bright-eyed and pink-cheeked. Halfway through the meal, Jeremy Round signalled him over to the table. 'Could we have another bottle of water, darling?' he asked, whereupon the pink cheeks reddened. The boy ran down the stairs to the bar. We heard sniggers from below. He was standing in the middle of a group of boys and girls pointing up at Jeremy and exclaiming, 'That man called me "darling". That man called me "darling".' Jeremy beamed.

At the end of dinner, Jeremy insisted on paying the bill. He handed the waiter a credit card, and when the youth returned with the chit, Jeremy put a couple of ten-pound notes on the plate with the words 'That's for you, darling.' 'Thank you, sir,' Darling spluttered. A phalanx of grinning waiters and waitresses watched as we left the premises.

On a hot summer morning, Jeremy and I drove to a town in Sussex to investigate a new restaurant. The car's roof was down, and we were enjoying the sunshine. There were roadworks in progress along several stretches of the route. Many of the labourers were stripped to the waist, and we eyed them appreciatively. Whenever the lights turned green Jeremy waved to the men, calling out, 'Goodbye, boys'. Some waved back, and one shouted 'Saucy' after us.

There were no leftovers when Jeremy came to dinner. It was an honour and pleasure to cook for him. I don't think I have ever met anyone with an appetite to match his. He wasn't a glutton, for his was a discerning palate. He knew exactly what he was eating, down to the minutest ingredient.

He exuded optimism, a sense that life was a series of exciting surprises, each one to be savoured to the full. He was restless when I knew him, anxious to be on the move. He often talked of the years he had spent in Turkey. He had learnt Turkish and mastered the cuisine. Now, in 1989, he was tired of England and bored at the prospect of being condemned to write solely about food. It was his intention to move to America, to drive across the entire continent, to make his name there. He had ambitions to be a poet and, perhaps, a novelist. He made this announcement for the future early in the year. Jeremy Trevathan would accompany him, share the adventure. I was saddened at the thought of losing such lively, entertaining company.

Along with a hundred others, I was to be saddened more seriously in August. I had been invited to attend a congress for food writers in Hong Kong, but declined for reasons of work. Jeremy went, and then travelled on to Macao. It was there that he died, in a hotel bathroom, of a brain haemorrhage. He had enjoyed his meal that evening. His last known words were: 'What time's breakfast?' His body was found in the morning, and the news relayed to his editor at the *Independent* in London. His parents, on a caravan holiday in France, were difficult to contact, and it was some days before they heard of their terrible loss. Jeremy was thirty-two.

Jeremy Trevathan flew to Macao to identify his friend, and to bring him back to England.

Jane Grigson and Elizabeth David were among the admirers who paid generous and heartfelt tributes to him. Elizabeth, with whom I was now friends, was especially devastated. She had always fought against the idea of having a biography written about her, but she changed her mind after reading, and subsequently meeting, Jeremy. Over lunch one day, she more or less appointed him her official biographer, taking pains to stress the reservations she had on the subject of biographical writing. That book would have been the greatest challenge yet for the young Jeremy, who was prepared to meet it. The cantankerous Elizabeth died in 1992, and two biographies – the first lively, but fanciful and inaccurate; the second worthily accurate but dull – have been published already. I can record with confidence that she would have loathed them.

Jeremy Round is the author of a solitary work. *The Independent Cook* is typically quirky and idiosyncratic, containing recipes from Turkey, the American South and North Africa, as well as France, Italy and Britain. He would have gone on to write even better books.

Some months after Jeremy's death, Jeremy Trevathan and I decided to live together. It was a sensible decision, and ten years of shared happiness and domestic contentment ensued. Jeremy exercised Circe at weekends, and the dog was pleased to have two masters.

Jeremy's calmness and common sense are qualities he has earned and worked at over many years. His parents divorced when he was six, and his childhood was spent in London, in Athens, in Puerto Rico and, partly, in his native America. People are startled to learn that he is American, because his voice – with its oddly appropriate Cornish burr – couldn't be less transatlantic.

Jeremy's stability is the more remarkable when one considers his itinerant upbringing. Yet I know of men and women who were raised in loving settled families who lack his steely strength of character in a crisis.

He basked in the light of Jeremy Round's brilliance. As so

often happens, only a handful of Round's friends kept in touch with him. Today he is a respected publisher, casting his own light for others to bask in.

We live apart now – in the flesh, at any rate. Our love has changed its course, but has not been diminished.

Siren

On a blustery morning in March 1985, I went to the market to buy a new sieve for the kitchen. But before I could fulfil this perfectly ordinary domestic task I became a changed man, almost in an instant. I should have walked past the pet shop, gone to the hardware store and returned home. I didn't, though. The sight of a solitary puppy compelled me to stop. I reminded myself that I was not, and never had been, a dog lover. Yet I continued to look at the pretty little honey-coloured collie in the window. I realized I was in danger of succumbing to its beauty.

I walked on. I bought the sieve. I enjoyed my favourite daily spectacle in Shepherd's Bush market – that of a group of Arab women, draped in black from head to toe, with only their eyes visible, buying countless pairs of knee-length under-wear, of the kind that were once called 'passion killers'. These particular 'passion killers' were in garish, even violent, colours – red, blue, green – and made of a material that crackled to the touch. I imagined rather esoteric orgies taking place at the embassy, as the women piled into the waiting, chauffeur-driven Bentley with their neon-lit knickers. 'Those girls keep me in business,' remarked the stallholder with a wink. 'Ours not to reason, mate.'

I stopped once more outside the pet shop. I admired the puppy for the last time. It would soon have an owner, I

reasoned. Others would find it irresistible. I left it to its happy
– I hoped – fate.

Two hours later, I entered the market, praying that the pet
shop window would be empty. The puppy was asleep on its
bed of straw and torn-up newspaper. I knew, now, that I was
lost. I knew that I was irretrievably lost when I heard myself
asking the price of the collie.

'She's not a thoroughbred,' the old Irishman who ran the
shop told me. 'You can have her for forty pounds.'

I got out my cheque book.

'I prefer cash. It's safer.'

I explained that I had to go to the bank and would be gone
for a while.

'She's yours. Don't worry. She'll be here for you.'

As I set off for the bank, I considered the possibility of not
returning to the shop, of being released from the madness I
was experiencing, of coming to my senses. I had neither the
time nor the energy to care for a dog. I was in the middle of
writing a long novel, *Gabriel's Lament*, and I was living with a
partner who was in poor health. I had the means of escape. I

was in thrall to a bundle of fur with bright brown eyes. I was behaving like a besotted fool. I listed all the reasons why I shouldn't part with forty pounds.

I heeded none of them. I handed over the money. I took the dog in my arms and soon she was licking my face, my ears, my neck. I was drenched in her pee as I carried her home, wondering what reception I might expect when I told David the obvious truth that I had fallen in love with a puppy.

'What's that?'

'It's a dog.'

'I can see it's a dog. What are you doing with it?'

'I bought her.'

'Take her back.'

'I can't.'

'Why not?'

'Because I can't bear to.'

'You have a book to write, you idiot.'

He was silent and morose for hours. He glowered at the dog as she peed and shat on the newspapers I had put down for her.

The silence continued through dinner and well into the evening. It was nearly midnight when David spoke.

'You can keep her under one condition.'

'What's that?'

'That you call her Circe. It's the right name for her. I hate to say it but she's an enchantress. And the flat smells absolutely disgusting.'

Dog Days

'You bought her. You clean up after her. She's your responsibility.'

In those first weeks following my momentous decision to
buy Circe there was a great deal of cleaning up to do. Every
floor in the flat was covered in newspapers, to accommodate
the various messes she was making. She wanted to eat everything, even – I discovered to my horror – the contents of the
cat's litter tray. I got her a wicker basket to sleep in, and the
taste and flavour of the wicker obviously appealed to her, for
it was soon reduced to shreds.

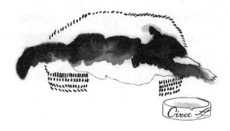

The cat, a sulky tortoiseshell named Alice, lived almost
permanently in the garden while Circe was confined to the
house. She hissed at her rival, who reacted with indifference
or frantic tail-wagging, depending on her mood. She was a
puppy and pleased with her young life. I would be pleased,
I knew, when it would be possible to take her to the park. I
yearned for that happy time. I had promised David that I

would have the carpets cleaned professionally the moment her necessary imprisonment was over. The stale smell lingering in every room would be expertly dispatched.

The vet, Michael Gordon – who shares my interest in, and admiration for, the writings of Primo Levi – saw Circe a second time and declared her fit and safe to meet other dogs. He advised me to mix vegetables in with her food. I followed that advice for sixteen years, feeding Circe once a day, in the early evening. She stayed lean and energetic as a result, unlike some of the lethargic animals she met on our travels.

The day of her freedom dawned, and I was yanked towards the park for the first of many times. She somehow knew it was there. There was some training to do along the way and she learnt very quickly that the pavement was not to be fouled. Within a week, she understood that she wouldn't be slapped or chided if she made for the gutter.

Catching her, bringing her to heel, was not so easy. I often needed the assistance of my fellow dog owners, who laughed as they attempted to catch hold of her. Circe was intent on staying free, especially in the winter when she ran faster to keep warm. I lived in terror that someone would leave the gate of the Dogs Only area open, thus ensuring her certain escape. And that is precisely what happened one morning. She sprinted off at an alarming speed, forgetting the ball I was throwing to her. I chased after her, bellowing her name. Fortunately for me, she caught sight of a luckless jogger and chose him as her target. She yapped as she ran beside him, and then – to the man's justifiable annoyance – tried to nip his ankle. He stopped and grabbed her by the back of the neck, and I took possession of her.

'Have you no control over that bloody thing?'

The truth was that I hadn't, and I was so grateful to the jogger that I couldn't contradict him.

'Not yet,' I said, panting. 'I'm very sorry.'

'So you bloody should be,' he snapped, recommencing his run.

I was suitably humbled, and dragged the uncomprehending offender home.

In Richmond Park, some weeks later, I let Circe off the lead so that my two godsons could play with her. Their parents, David and I sat on the grass drinking white wine and eating smoked salmon. We watched the boys taking turns to throw the ball, and smiled with delight at Circe's impatience when they teased her by holding on to it a little too long for her liking. The game was proceeding happily until a running man hove into view. And he really was running, not jogging. Circe saw him and found it impossible to resist the thrill of pursuit. The man was listening to music through earphones and was oblivious to her barking. I gave chase and ran like a demon for twenty minutes while the long-distance runner and Circe forged ahead. It was she who stopped on this occasion, having worn herself out with the effort of scampering alongside a man who ignored her.

She remained on the lead for the rest of the afternoon – to her, and the boys', irritation. And I, at the age of forty-seven, had taken sufficient exercise in the blazing heat of late July.

'You don't frighten her. She's got you where she wants you. She owns you, not the other way round.'

I shouted at her when I was angry, and she frequently continued to disobey me. Neither David nor my great friend

Vanni Bartolozzi had cause to shout. Their voices, seldom raised, had bass notes she listened to with apprehension. They told her she was doing wrong, and she believed them.

Mongrel Goddess

'What's his name?'

The question was asked first when she was an energetic puppy, propelling me along the street in her desperate need to reach the park. *His* name was still being enquired after in her lively old age. People assume that all dogs are male, until informed otherwise.

'Her name is Circe.'

'Susie? That's nice.'

Some, children mostly, heard me correctly.

'*Sir-sea. Sir-sea.* Who's she?'

She was a Greek goddess – some say a witch – who lured Odysseus, the great hero at the siege of Troy, on to her island. She turned at least half of his sailors into swine.

'Pigs,' I translated.

'Why did she do that?'

'Only she could tell you. It was in her nature, I suppose.'

'Can she turn me into a pig?' the ten-year-old wondered.

'You're that already,' his older sister responded.

The impatient Circe wanted an end to this tiresome conversation, and pulled vigorously on her lead.

'We have to go. Goodbye.'

'Goodbye, *Sir-sea*,' the boy and girl chanted, and then giggled. They were to become, as they got older, two of her most devoted admirers. They told their mother, who was greatly amused, that they knew a dog – she looked like Lassie – who could turn men into pigs.

'Was it just sailors, Mister?' The boy needed clarification. 'Or was it anybody?'

'In the story it's just sailors.'

'That's a relief,' said their mother, giving a mock sigh. 'Your dad's safe, then. I was ever so frightened for him, in case he should bump into – what's her name?'

'It's *Sir-sea*,' the daughter was quick to tell her.

'She really does look like Lassie. Come on, you two, you'll be late for school.'

Circe reacted with disdain or incomprehension when addressed as Lassie. She was aware of the name she had been given, and duly answered to it. (The original Lassie, in *Lassie Come Home* and other movies, was a dog. His genitals were trussed up and his hindquarters cosmeticized, Hollywood fashion.) She allowed herself to be patted and stroked, always, by those who called her Lassie, without bothering to find out if she was known by something else.

'She's not Lassie,' I would say, when I could be bothered to. 'Lassie was a thoroughbred. She isn't.'

A snooty woman had reminded me of her mongrel's status when Circe was about nine months old and not growing to be quite as tall as the average border collie.

'I think you should know,' she boomed, striding across the grass to where I was throwing the ball for Circe to retrieve, 'that your bitch is neither a sheltie nor a collie. Did you part with money for her?'

'I did.'

'You were swindled.'

'It wasn't very much.'

'I should hope not,' she snorted, walking off with her pedigree Labrador.

Swindled? For forty pounds? Here was the canine class system at its deadly work. My beautiful hybrid, my intelligent bitch, hadn't been interbred to the point of idiocy. She was her own mistress, and I was – at certain gullible times – her willing Odysseus, ready to have myself tied to the mast on her silent instructions.

'She's a mongrel,' the woman remarked contemptuously, slamming the gate behind her.

'So are you,' I shouted. 'So are we all.'

I was to listen to this animal fascism – purity of the breed stuff and nonsense – very rarely in the sixteen years of Circe's life. David had been astute to detect a Circean quality in her, for not all domestic animals, in common with all human beings, have the power to enchant.

'Your dog's smiling,' was a frequent observation.

And it was true. She was baring her teeth without menace, without anger. She was displaying them, benevolently, to whomever was delighting in her charm.

Mercurial

David spent almost a year in Circe's exuberant company. Whenever he felt well enough, he would come to the park and watch as she evaded capture with all the quick-witted brilliance and energy at her command.

Between May 1985 and January 1986 he re-created the miracle of Lazarus (without Christ's assistance, but rather with the dedicated skills of the men and women in the Intensive Care Unit at Westminster Hospital) no fewer than four times. He was not prepared to make a fifth attempt at surviving, and died towards the end of March. Another return from the beyond was not even to be contemplated.

We were introduced to each other in the summer of 1964, and by the end of the year we were sharing a flat on the top floor of a Victorian house in Paddington, previously owned by the notorious pimp and shady property developer Peter Rachman. David was working in the wardrobe at the Royal Opera House, Covent Garden, and I was at Harrods, no longer resting between acting engagements. My theatrical career, such as it was, was over.

David had once tried to dye his hair with a product that burnt his forelocks away. He had green eyes that darted with happy mischief or ferocious anger. He was small and slightly built, yet he had the power to terrify bullies or thugs. He had exquisite manners when he wasn't incensed by someone's boorish or grand behaviour. I remember an evening when a famous poet and his wife invited us to dinner. The other guests were a charming French journalist and Kingsley Amis and his then wife, Elizabeth Jane Howard. Amis was in a foul mood, insisting on eating eggs, bacon and sausage instead of the 'foreign muck' being prepared. The poet's wife was in a tizzy in the basement kitchen. When she came into the sitting room looking flustered, Amis quipped, 'You must be stewing something in Albanian goat's piss to judge by the smell.' On the instant David said, 'That was bloody rude, Mr Amis. I think you should apologize.'

Amis mumbled a few words and fell silent.

I had met the famous poet when David and I were still living in our Paddington eyrie. He had been kind to me, praising my early novels, and he would later secure me a well-paid job at the universities of Newcastle and Durham, where I was writer in residence. By way of expressing my gratitude, I invited him and his wife to dine with us, for David was an excellent and inventive cook. They duly arrived, climbing the six flights of stairs that led to the flat. They walked into our tiny sitting room, and the poet's wife stared at the pictures, the ornaments, the furniture. Then, ignoring her hosts and turning to her husband, she exclaimed, 'Just think, darling, only two nights ago we were in New York with Igor and Véra.'

We were too stunned by this lofty put-down to enquire which Igor and which Véra she was referring to. It says much for David's graciousness that on the night of the Albanian goat's piss witticism he came to the wife's aid at the stove, rescuing the meal she was preparing for those not averse to foreign food. He was to regret this act of simple decency, as I shall relate.

David had trained to be a classical dancer, but his looks and height meant that he would be confined to character roles. He was told by his teacher, Elsa Brunelleschi, that he could never be a *danseur noble*. He was, briefly, a chorus boy at the London Palladium, attracting several sugar daddies, who took him for supper at the Savoy Grill or the Café de Paris. His expertise as a tailor and cutter, with a faultless eye for what looked natural on a dancer, singer or actor, ensured him a job at the Royal Opera House, where he was healthily disrespectful to the stars and designers who treated the staff as menials.

He displayed his republican mettle whenever Princess Margaret attended the dress rehearsal of a new ballet. Her Royal Highness sat in the stalls, with a lackey or two beside her to light her cigarettes and top up her glass with whisky. Anyone passing in front of her was required to bow or curtsey, as often as a dozen or more times. David refused to bow, explaining to his boss that to do so would be to waste precious minutes. The success of the show did not depend on the presence of the royal dwarf, he reasoned. I cherish this memory of him, the sole person at Covent Garden who refused to toady to the privileged martinet, smoking where others could not smoke, drinking where mere mortals could not drink. She was lucky. If he *had* bowed – or curtsied – he would have let out, in one form or another, an appropriate raspberry. Some are born not to bow or scrape, and he was of their exalted number.

It was his close friend Jean who kept me informed about David's small, but necessary, acts of rebellion. Jean, who somehow managed to fend off the unsubtle advances of a famously randy tenor and the very specific sexual requirements of a great bass from Bulgaria, revealed that David had ordered Rudolf Nureyev to take a long shower with lots of soap before he, David, would continue with the fitting. 'You stink, Rudi,' he complained. 'And your jockstrap is disgusting.' The startled Nureyev complied, returning in half an hour, smelling fresh and sporting a clean truss. 'That's better, isn't it? We can both breathe now, can't we, Rudi?'

David was at Covent Garden when the Kirov Ballet performed in the summer of 1966. He went into the lavatory one morning and was struck by the sight of a handsome Russian dancer clutching his penis in a state of obvious anxiety. 'Help' was the only word the man seemed able to speak. The penis, David saw, was inflamed. 'Interpreter,' David remarked, whereupon the dancer gestured wildly to indicate that the interpreter, who was also Russian and a member of the company, must not know about his problem. The dancer zipped up his fly and followed David into the corridor, where David found his boss and explained that the Russian had the clap and must be treated at a nearby hospital. Outside the Opera House he flagged down a taxi and told the driver to take them to St Thomas's. The Russian was making little moaning noises, and David patted his arm to assure him that all would be well.

They sat in the waiting room of the 'special clinic' for what seemed hours before David insisted that his friend, who was dancing at the Opera House that evening, should be seen by a doctor. The anguished Russian was examined. He had gonorrhoea. The word was written on a scrap of paper for him, and he shook his head in bewilderment. He was given an injection of penicillin. David accompanied him to the underground 'special clinic' on three more occasions, and when the Kirov were due to leave the grateful dancer embraced him to the point of breathlessness and kissed him on both cheeks. 'You friend. You good friend. You give me help.'

David's father was a drunk, a womanizer and a spendthrift. Major Healy was stationed in South Africa at the start of the Second World War, and David and his brother Arthur grew up in Amanzimtoti, near Durban, cared for by a black nanny whom they adored. Their mother, Adza, hated the socializing duties expected of an army wife, and tried for a while to ignore her husband's constant infidelities. The couple returned to Britain in the late 1940s, and divorced in the following decade. Major Healy disappeared from their lives, only to reappear at the stage door of the London Palladium after a performance in which his eldest son had been 'hoofing'.

'I'm your dad, David. Don't you recognize me?'

'Yes.'

'I'm on my uppers, David. Can you lend your old dad a fiver?'

'No.'

That was to be their last meeting. The major's demand for money and the sentimental reminder that he was his 'old dad' caused David considerable misery, even though he turned the encounter into a comic anecdote. I think this was the reason he was happiest in the company of women, especially those who were having trouble with men. His 'dad' came to represent everything he despised in a certain kind of heterosexual man – the kind who regard their wives or lovers as a subspecies, available at all times in either the bedroom or the kitchen.

Adza was brought up as a Roman Catholic but alienated her devout relatives when she married the major, who called himself a Protestant. She was cut off by the Williams family, who were Irish despite the Welsh name. After her divorce, her cousins contacted her, letting her know that her marriage hadn't really been a marriage in the eyes of the one true church. Now she was free to marry a Catholic, who would raise her boys in the faith. Adza, who was now living in Abergavenny, chose another Protestant as her second husband. This was too much for her cousins, aunts and uncles, who informed her in a single, outraged letter – signed by them all – that she would not be welcomed if she had the nerve to turn up in Dublin.

Adza was petite and pretty in a doll-like way. She bore a close physical resemblance to the writer Jean Rhys. She dressed elegantly on modest means, a knack her eldest son inherited. Although her second Protestant husband, George, was a retired labourer, Adza still acted like the major's wife she once was. She considered my sister, who spoke with a pronounced Cockney accent, 'frightfully common'.

George's false teeth were rarely in his mouth. He was comfortable with his puckered appearance. Every visitor to the family bathroom was confronted by his Everest of a denture, gleaming unnaturally white in a glass on the shelf above the washbasin. Adza was always chiding him to put the teeth where they belonged, and he invariably responded that his gums were strong enough to chew the roast beef he loved to eat.

George reminded me of Joe Gargery, the honest and sweet-natured blacksmith in *Great Expectations*. Like Joe, he was not at ease in 'polite company' and like Joe, too, he found London an intimidating place. The traffic unnerved him, and so did the crowds. The tall, gangling man (he was well over six feet) had to depend on his tiny wife to guide him through the bustling city streets.

They stayed with us for a long weekend and gladly accepted my mother's invitation to Sunday lunch. I warned them that her lunches were mountainous, and George expressed pleasure at the prospect. We took a taxi to Battersea, with Adza hoping that George hadn't been teasing her when he said he had lost his teeth. It wasn't until we were on the doorstep of my mother's house that George removed the denture from his jacket pocket and popped it into his mouth. The effect was startling. The mouth was hugely expanded, the sculpted molars rendering him incapable of comprehensible speech. His tongue was trapped behind them. He was suddenly a ghoul, with a ghoul's smile to match.

Joan, my sister, opened the front door. She was transfixed by George's smiling teeth, the like of which she had never seen. Introductions were made, and the five of us proceeded up the stairs to the second-floor landing where my mother was waiting anxiously. She sensed immediately that the diminutive Adza, in her picture hat and tasteful summer dress, was a woman of a certain class and said 'How do you do?' and 'Pleased to meet you' in the voice she assumed for her wealthy or titled employers. Adza, having winced at my sister's dropped aitches and elongated vowels, shook hands with a kindred spirit. George, looming behind her, tried to say something but could only manage a strangled noise that ended in a whistle.

We went into the rarely opened front room. The cutlery gleamed on the dining table, which was covered with a pristine, lace-trimmed cloth. Adza sat down daintily, accepting the gin and tonic she was offered and sipping it with exaggerated finesse. George merited a fierce glare from his wife as he guzzled his beer, the porcelain blockade causing him to splutter.

The rib of beef my mother had prepared was accompanied by roast potatoes, cauliflower in a white sauce, peas, runner beans and glazed onions. There was gravy, of course, in the pretty Victorian gravy boat that only appeared at Christmas or on special occasions. We sat down to eat. The teeth were now giving George agonies of embarrassment as he attempted, and failed, to employ them for chewing. They clacked together and the meat fell back on to the plate.

'How can I put that poor man out of his misery?' my mother asked me in a whisper in the kitchen. 'He looks like a carthorse with those bloody great gnashers stuck in his face.'

'This is delicious, Mrs Bailey,' Adza remarked as my mother finally seated herself at the table.

'I hope there's enough.' This was her constant hope, constantly voiced.

'No, there isn't, Maudie,' David quipped. 'Where are the carrots? And what have you done with the cabbage?'

George's continuing agony was more than my mother could bear. 'Don't stand on ceremony, George.' (She called him George because she couldn't cope with his surname, Llewellyn.) 'Why don't you make yourself comfortable? Those teeth are a hindrance, aren't they? Why don't you take them out?'

Never was a denture removed with such speed, such keenness. At last we could hear what George was saying. 'Thank you, Mrs Bailey,' he enunciated. 'I can enjoy your food now.' And enjoy it he did, scooping up several helpings, his gums disposing of the meat, vegetables and three large portions of sherry trifle and custard. Adza's fury was barely contained, though she contrived to wear a dulcet smile whenever my mother drew her into conversation. The hated denture was in a handkerchief, in his pocket, and there it remained for the rest of that long summer afternoon.

A year or so afterwards, Adza began to exhibit the symptoms of the cruel disease, Huntington's chorea, that would kill her. The patient, devoted George held the cup to her lips so she could drink the tea he brewed for her. Her hands were in a perpetual tremor. Her speech became impaired, and a look of total helplessness seemed permanently set on her once-pretty features. Her life ended in dementia, though the last words to the younger son who was at her bedside suggest she had retained some of her wits: 'I want David here, not you,' she declared forcefully. Arthur, thinking that David would be pleased to hear how much Adza needed him, informed his brother of her parting message when he arrived later that day. David was torn apart. The train from London had stopped many times in open countryside, and he had missed his connection. She had been dead for hours when he reached the hospital. He was to relive that nightmarish journey, and its desolate conclusion, on various occasions in the years to come. The words 'I want David here, not you' assumed the quality of a curse for him, a terrible reminder of his inadequacy as the favourite son. I once heard him say it in his sleep.

'God moves in a mysterious way . . .' The news of Adza's death somehow reached Dublin. David received a black-bordered card with a gold cross in the centre. Inside was the message that Adza was now in the Catholic heaven where she belonged. The Williams family were praying for her immortal soul, and X-number (I forget how many) Hail Marys had been said.

David tore the card into pieces, which he then threw into the lavatory bowl. He pissed on them before flushing them away.

The final humiliation came in the form of a letter, banged out on an ancient typewriter with a superannuated ribbon, from a Dublin solicitor. I read it out to him. It transpired that an uncle had opened a trust fund for David and Arthur, the money to be paid to them when Adza was restored to the faith. Now that she was gone to rest it was safe to assume that she was with her Catholic forebears. A cheque for £3,500 was enclosed.

'Tear it up,' David shrieked.

I reminded him, calmly, that he owed a couple of thousand pounds in income tax. I advised him to sign the back of the cheque, making it payable to the Inland Revenue. He did so, and never heard from Dublin again.

Elsa, David's dance teacher, lived with her sister Lila in a house in Bayswater that had been built specifically for one of Queen Victoria's more favoured servants. They spent most of every day in the kitchen, where Lila toiled contentedly at the stove, surrounded by a succession of mangy cats. The sisters disapproved of vets and doctors, believing that nature knew best and that medical assistance was necessary only in extreme circumstances. The flea-ridden creatures would slink in from the wild, overgrown garden in absolute confidence that food was there for the miaowing. They would leap on to the table on which Lila was rolling pastry or stuffing a chicken and be certain of a tasty titbit. 'Is *angelita* hungry?' The question had only one answer, as the cats demonstrated each time it was asked. If two or more were present, it was left to Elsa to separate them, sometimes with a broom handle, as they pounced on the scraps Lila tossed in their direction.

Lila had a serene, even temper, which perfectly comple-mented Elsa's tendency to overdramatize the mildest upset. Lila cared nothing for appearances, especially her own. She made no effort to get rid of facial hair, and a tooth that suddenly fell out was never replaced. Elsa wore elaborate jewellery – vast hoops of earrings – and applied mascara, powder and vivid scarlet lipstick in a manner that became ever more slapdash as she got older.

Lila was a brilliant and eccentric cook. She had hundreds of recipes at her command. The various liqueurs that relatives sent or brought back from Argentina were seldom drunk – 'This will give the dish a kick' – but rather used as exotic flavourings for the cakes and biscuits she was always baking. I watched her closely one December afternoon as she made a chocolate gâteau. Into the large bowl she flung flour, butter, caster sugar. An *angelita* appeared beside her. She stroked it tenderly, and then put her hand back into the bowl. She picked up a brown bottle and poured its entire contents into the mixture. 'For the kick,' she explained. I was to remember the floury hand on the cat's arched back when my sister requested a second slice of the chocolate cake on Christmas morning, declaring it the most delicious she had ever eaten.

We were gathered in the state apartments, as the sisters described the dining room, that Christmas. The dining table could accommodate twenty people. A heavy iron chandelier dominated the room. The furniture was of dark, solid wood. It might have been the setting for a play by Lorca – except that these two sisters had satisfied desires the wretched daughters of Bernarda Alba were forbidden to experience. Elsa had mixed the drinks in anticipation of the guests' arrival – gins and tonic; whiskies and soda. In her anxiety to discover if she had got the measure right, she had taken a sip from every glass, each one of which bore a sizeable trace of her scarlet lipstick. My fastidious mother could not conceal the disgust she felt when Elsa handed her a gin. In common with everyone else, she drank from the unstained side of the glass, though at a moment when Elsa was out of sight she dipped into her handbag and produced a tissue with which she wiped the rim.

Elsa and Lila were frequent guests at the Royal Opera House on ballet nights. They sat in the centre stalls, in aisle seats. Elsa wore a long green evening dress and pearls and earrings, while Lila dressed in discreet black. In winter, both donned furs. They refused to eat or drink in either the stalls bar or the Crush Bar, finding the prices exorbitant. So they took their dinner with them, in a picnic basket and a bedraggled shopping bag. They were not, it has to be said, popular with the balletgoers sitting near them, who had to step over the picnic basket and endure the smell of hard-boiled eggs after the first interval. They ate cold meats and salads, and drank red wine and hot coffee from a Thermos flask. The meal lasted until the curtain calls, and sometimes beyond. Elsa was in the habit of muttering obscenities in Spanish if a dancer or choreographer displeased her, and those in the audience who understood the meaning of *coño de puta* were either amused or shocked. Regular patrons were inclined to ask at the box office if they could be kept at a safe distance from those two 'appalling old women', one of whom refused to be silenced, even after threat of being removed from the theatre. Elsa and Lila were, as my sister noted appreciatively, 'proper characters'.

Elsa was returning to bed one night with a glass of milk

when she heard a curious sound coming from the state apartments. Her decision not to investigate probably saved her life, for the noise she heard was of the chandelier hitting the dining table. It had proved too weighty to hold for the burglars who had unscrewed it from the ceiling, and the sisters were to see it the following day, embedded in the ruined table, amid other wreckage. The thieves had been thwarted, and in their frustration and haste to leave they stole an album containing photographs of parents, brothers, uncles, aunts and cousins. The loss of these precious souvenirs upset Elsa and Lila deeply, motivated as their theft was by spite, not gain. The men also took some gold doubloons – family heirlooms, beyond value.

It had rained steadily before and after the burglary. Lila, venturing into the garden, chanced upon the tools the men had used to break into the house. They were covered in mud. She picked them up and carried them into the kitchen and washed them at the sink. Then she dried and polished them clean with a towel, little realizing that she had got rid of incriminating fingerprints along with the mud. The police were not pleased when she presented them with what she referred to as the 'evidence'.

In the years of our friendship with Elsa and Lila, David and I lived happily – if somewhat histrionically – in the flat in Paddington. My first and second novels were published, and David left Covent Garden to work as a freelance costumier. (He loathed the word 'costume', which suggested something arcane and dead to him. He produced period clothes for living people.) The minute dining room became his increasingly cluttered workroom, for he loved to function in seeming chaos. I had daily employment too, as a reader for my publisher Jonathan Cape. The phrase 'proud breasts' appeared in one trashy spy novel after another, all written under the influence of Ian Fleming. 'Why are the breasts always proud?' I asked my fellow reader, William Plomer. 'Ah,' he replied, 'I think it's because they're imposing. The girls' mothers had to eat snoek, a distinctly fatty fish, during the war, and that may explain why the breasts have this stuck-up appearance. Blame their pride on snoek.'

David's reputation as a costumier was at its highest then. His particular delight was in making clothes that fitted naturally and comfortably on operatic divas, and singers such as Montserrat Caballé, Shirley Verrett, Janet Baker, Beverley Sills and Teresa Stratas climbed the six flights to see him. The neighbours were impressed by the Bentleys and Rolls Royces waiting below. 'You need a corset,' he assured Caballé, who had given her measurements as 46, 46 and 46. She spluttered in protest that she had never worn, and would never wear, such a horrible object. 'I will build you a corset in which you can sing freely,' he guaranteed. She went on protesting until the hour of the fitting, when she looked in the mirror and saw that he had given her a waist. What's more, she could breathe easily in the light contraption he had designed. 'You have made a fat little Spanish girl very happy,' she cooed, kissing him warmly on both cheeks.

David's greatest asset in those days, apart from his admired talent as a tailor and cutter, was his honesty. He saw no reason to flatter or suck up to the artists he held in esteem. If a colour didn't suit the singer's complexion or physique, he advised her to resist it. He worked on a basis of mutual pride and respect, and was only disconcerted on those rare occasions when he was treated as a menial. Yet, deep down, he was aware that however well he had fulfilled the designer's intentions (and sometimes he was able to interpret a sqiggle pretending to be a sketch) it was not enough to make his name, David Healy, known beyond a small, incestuous circle.

I made the acquaintance of other writers – most notably Angus Wilson, who had introduced me to Elizabeth Bowen and been characteristically kind, and Iris Murdoch, whom I had met on a tour of the Midlands organized by the Arts Council. One night, in Knutsford – the origin of Mrs Gaskell's Cranford – an overdressed woman in the front room of the church hall announced that she hadn't heard of the three men on the panel but simply adored Miss Murdoch's novels. 'Why is that?' Iris demanded, out of curiosity. 'Oh, because they're so predictable,' the woman replied. 'That isn't much of a compliment,' Iris snapped. The woman was relentless in her misplaced enthusiasm. 'I mean, I feel so at home in them. You seem to have written them with me in mind. I always know where I am.' This was insupportable to Iris, who muttered 'Stupid cow' under her breath and invited a sensible question from somebody else.

Iris was to use that expression again, at a party she gave in her London pied-à-terre. A rather butch ex-nun was telling anyone who could be cajoled into listening that she was now a painter. She wore a smock for emphasis. She had doubts about her new vocation. 'Is there any point in painting after Titian?' she wondered aloud to everybody she met. Before one could respond with a reasoned 'Well . . .' she had answered the question herself: 'Of course there isn't.' As she became more and more drunk, the rhetorical question took on a defiant note. 'Is there any point in painting,' she boomed, 'after Titian?' I seem to recall a brave soul quietly remarking that Rembrandt and Goya came after Titian, but she was drowned out with an assertive 'Of course there isn't.' Two hours later, when it was time to leave, the painter was reeling, and still muttering the name of Titian. We were standing in the hall-way, saying our goodbyes to Iris, when the painter, pointing at a bowl of red roses, exclaimed: 'What beautiful flowers, Iris. Who gave them to you?' The reply was immediate, and brusque: 'You did, you stupid cow.'

In 1976, I went to live in America, where I remained for almost three years. In the summer of 1977, Iris invited David to her annual party. He arrived in some trepidation, not being at ease among intellectuals. The small flat was crammed with people, none of whom he recognized. It was then, with some relief, that he noticed the famous poet and his wife in a far corner. He made his way towards them and said hello. The poet, looking down on him, asked 'Do we know you?' and David answered yes. He reminded the couple that they had dined with us in our first flat, and then how he had rescued the wife's meal when the taunts of Mr Amis had driven her into a state of near-panic. These calmly pronounced reminders made no impression on the pair, who began scanning the company for someone else to talk to. David walked away from them and out of the party.

(I had assumed, wrongly it seems, that David had told them, in very precise Anglo-Saxon terms, where to get off. A friend who was lodging in our Hammersmith house at the time assures me that David returned home early in a state of shock and disbelief. He had been wounded by their snubbing of him, offended deeply by their haughty rudeness. He had left them in silence, his dignity intact.)

'I hear enough about books and writers,' David would declare, on opening the front door to Angus (always accompanied by his companion, Tony Garrett) or to Iris (who often came alone). Since the other guests were not literary types, the conversation ranged over a variety of topics. Iris never cared to talk about herself or her work, and was happy to ask questions, beginning with 'And what do you do?' Angus, by contrast, adored being the centre of attention, and allowed David to tease him and even, on one occasion, tell him he was talking bollocks. 'I do like your wicked friend,' Angus once confided. 'But he's bad for me. He makes me feel so *camp*.'

I remember two dinner parties made hellish by the self-importance of authors. Both occurred towards the end of David's life, when his cooking was unsurpassable. I had admired a certain biographer for many years, but nothing in her writing prepared us for the onslaught of egoism we were subjected to that night. She made no comment on the food David had prepared with such devoted skill, and assumed he was a hired chef, to judge by her parting words to me. She arrived late, barged into the sitting room and demanded, in stentorian tones, if anyone present knew anything about death by drowning. A stunned silence ensued. It was her theory – a theory that dominated the conversation for virtually the whole evening – that Virginia Woolf had not committed suicide. *Au contraire* – Leonard had murdered her, dragged her body down to the river, weighted it with stones (the very stones found in her pockets) and ditched it into the water. It made sense, she maintained, at length. Leonard was Jewish and his wife famously anti-Semitic. What better reason had he for killing her?

That evening, however, was – in retrospect – a mere fore-taste of the horror to come. An old and dear friend of mine had developed an interest in the copious writings of an American named May Sarton, a tireless diarist, autobiographer, novelist and poet. She and Sarton had corresponded, and a friendship of sorts had begun. I was in Nairn, in the far north of Scotland, working on the opening chapters of my novel *Gabriel's Lament* when a parcel containing a selection from Sarton's vast output arrived. I took time off from writing to read a novel – I have forgotten the title though not, alas, the content – about an elderly woman being placed in an institution. I found the book insufferably sentimental. The central character is a saintly victim in a world of cruel doctors and nurses. My own first novel, *At the Jerusalem*, is concerned with an irritable and irritating widow coping with life in a home, surrounded by people who are neither saints nor demons. I phoned my dear friend and asked her what crime I had perpetrated to merit the punishment of having to read such twaddle. She advised me to turn to the diaries. I did so, but not for long. I soon wearied of details of book-signings and meetings with her devoted readers, who were all women and mostly lesbian. There were no insights into the work of other writers, and the bland prose was completely devoid of those charm-free asides that inform the liveliest published diaries – like those of the composer Ned Rorem, for example, who finds space in the latest entertaining volumes to savage each new work by his self-appointed rival Elliott Carter.

Four months before Circe came into our lives, May Sarton turned up in London to give a talk to her women admirers and sign copies of her recent books. My old friend, knowing my views on all matters Sartonian, was nevertheless pleased when David and I suggested that she invite Sarton and her travelling companion to dinner. I bought a brace of pheasants from the butcher we patronized in Soho. (Reg, who always served me, was in the habit of saying, during the game season, 'Hello, Paul, do you fancy a large cock?' The other customers at the counter were often startled by this question and by my enthusistic reply in the affirmative.)

I feel somewhat like Conrad's Marlow, the measured remembrancer of futility and despair, as I think back to that grim November evening. The chain-smoking, hard-drinking Sarton was in a belligerent mood from the outset. I had been told of her fondness for Scotch whisky, and duly filled a tumbler for her. She dispatched it down her throat with surprising speed. Her companion Edythe (felicitous spelling) drank moderately and said very little because Sarton gave her no opportunity to express anything as controversial as an opinion. My old friend tried to ease the tension that was steadily building up.

Introductions were made. The already tipsy Sarton mistook Lisa, the actress who lived on the ground floor, for a novelist, and assumed that I was an actor. The full nature of her confusion struck me when I expressed cautious enthusiasm for the writer Jayne Anne Phillips, whose first collection of short stories I had just read. 'Nobody takes the literary judgements of actors seriously,' she declared. I was too astonished to continue.

David listened intently as the diarist launched herself into a litany of self-praise. We heard that May Sarton was more than a mere novelist or poet. Sackloads of letters from lonely women reached her home in Maine by every post, and she replied to each one *personally*.

Breaking the silence that followed these revelations, she turned to Lisa and enquired, 'What kind of books do you write?'

Lisa laughed, and said she was an actress, and that I was the writer in the house.

'You're not an actor?' The gruff voice sounded angry for some unaccountable reason.

'I was. A long time ago. I'm a novelist.'

It had taken almost an hour to establish this. I wondered if, from now on, any literary judgement I might venture would be treated seriously, not cursorily dismissed. In one of her volumes of autobiography, Sarton had boasted of a night of sexual – and presumably drunken – euphoria with Elizabeth Bowen. I mentioned, casually, that I had met the great author at a party shortly before her death. I had been tongue-tied in her presence, but she was gracious and charming in the face of my awkwardness as she sat on the sofa in the publisher's office in Soho.

'I knew Elizabeth *very well*,' Sarton announced. 'Very well indeed.'

That was another show-stopper. Sarton's proffered glass was refilled. It was clear to me that she wanted us to praise her writing. I am no stranger to deviousness, but I have never been able to pretend to admire work I consider second-rate. It does not follow that an inferior writer must of necessity be an inferior person. I had hoped, against the written evidence, that Sarton would prove to be interesting at least. Fond hope.

We sat down to eat. Edythe praised the smoked salmon mousse, which Sarton picked at. She was now consuming wine with the same fervour she had applied to the whisky. Trouble seemed to be looming with each intake. She had begun to glower. She offered no comment on the pheasant, which Edythe again was the first to praise, but complained instead of the terrible burden she had to fulfil by responding *personally* to the thousands of letters she received every year. There were days when she had no time for her own work.

'When I get back to Maine, there'll be hundreds of the damned things waiting for me.'

'I've only read two of your books,' Lisa remarked. 'I can't understand why so many people write to you or why you have to reply to them.'

Sarton, enraged, banged both fists on the table.

'If you'd bothered to read the other forty, you would understand,' she bellowed.

'Could we keep the decibels down a little?' David asked, while Sarton snorted.

'Shut up,' she shouted, glowering at Lisa. 'I'm talking. You're only the cook.'

The moment I had dreaded had come. But David surprised me. He took off his apron and placed it carefully on the back of a chair. He walked over to the dining table and looked straight at Sarton, who was still fuming. He spoke quietly but firmly.

'You are without doubt the rudest, the most egotistical, monstrous human being I have ever met.'

'He doesn't like me,' Sarton wailed, her gravelly voice sounding almost girlish.

David went downstairs and phoned a close friend, whom he regaled with a detailed report on the behaviour of our guest of honour.

I served the dessert. 'It's delicious,' said the ever-placatory Edythe.

Sarton pushed the plate away from her. She was in need of the last word, and here it came, deafeningly. 'I get the impression that no one in this house likes writers.'

It was impossible for David not to hear this. 'Too fucking right,' he called up the stairwell.

It was time for Sarton and Edythe to go, even though the proud author of forty books was spoiling for a real fight. My friend rang for a taxi, which came in ten minutes, to the relief of everybody but the disgruntled writer. Lisa and I said goodbye to Edythe, and tried to say goodbye to May Sarton, but she was muttering to herself and swaying from the drink she had knocked back with such determination.

'I feared something like this would happen,' Edythe confided in my old friend as they descended the stairs to the street.

We had a post-mortem. Had David met Sarton five years earlier, he would have frogmarched her out of the house. He could laugh now, which he did as the four of us repeated the various slights and insults Sarton had bestowed on the company for nearly three hours.

Sarton sent me a Christmas card, with one of her execrable poems on the back. She thanked a fellow writer for a memorable meal. The cook had been ignored once again. That she hadn't registered, in her self-absorption, what the kindly Edythe had clearly seen – that the man who cooked the dinner was terminally ill – is a horrible fact which continues to shock me. She hadn't noticed his gaunt eyes and sunken cheeks. Her mind was on those letters that had to be answered *personally*.

David's oldest and staunchest friend, Bill Pashley, told me recently of their first meeting in the late 1950s. David was working as a barman in a gay club called The Calabash, which was situated – until it was raided by the police and closed – in a back street in South Kensington. Bill was sitting in the club one evening chatting to an acquaintance when he saw that the voluble young man behind the bar was making everybody laugh.

'Who's he?' Bill asked.

'I wouldn't have anything to do with him, if I were you. He's *dangerous.*'

It was that single word – 'dangerous' – that drew Bill to David. He went across to the bar and introduced himself. Bill's self-deprecating humour and gift for recognizing and then mocking pomposity and pretentiousness greatly appealed to David, whose own talent for trenchant piss-taking was similar to his.

Bill, who now makes wedding dresses for the daughters of the titled and wealthy, only once shared a workroom with David. That once was more than enough. David created an atmosphere about him that was electric, nothing less, and Bill's placid temperament couldn't cope with it. Others could, and for them it was a source of inspiration, a challenge to give of their best.

'Are you always so charming, or is today a special occasion?' This was his standby question, delivered with an ingratiating smile, in the face of downright rudeness. He employed it for as long as I knew him, and I delighted in watching the reactions of those to whom it was addressed. People who make a habit of being insulting to their supposed inferiors tend not to have a capacity for self-deflation, and it was with a certain keen pleasure that I became aware how many of them actually thought they *were* charming, believing what David had said to be true.

David and I went about our different sexual ways eventually, but continued to live together. I still laugh when I remember his simple, but invariably successful, seduction technique.

'Have you ever thought of having your trousers hand-made?'
he would remark, *en passant*, to the policeman – he specialized
in policemen – or taxi driver, or labourer he had invited in for
the ubiquitous 'quick coffee'. The reply was always the same.
'I couldn't afford it, mate. Don't have that kind of money.'

'My prices are very reasonable. Why don't I measure you
anyway?'

Then he produced the tape measure, rather like a magician
surprised to see a rabbit in his hat, and a few minutes of careful
measuring would lead to the desired goal.

I was alone in the house when a woman from the wardrobe
department at BBC Television phoned. She needed a piece of
material urgently. She described it to me – the precise colour
and pattern – and I went into his cluttered workroom to search
for it. I did find it, and the woman said she would send a
courier to pick it up. I also found something else that day –
the evidence of his serious, private drinking. Underneath the
scattered piles of silks and cottons were dozens of empty gin
bottles, mostly miniatures. Why hadn't he thrown them out
with the rubbish? Had he wanted me to discover them?

He lived in fear of contracting Huntington's chorea, and
steadily killed himself in the process. It took a long time for
his work to deteriorate, and when it did he was too blinded
by gin to understand why no one was phoning him, apart
from a couple of loyal friends who gave him the odd, relatively
small, commission.

He had money troubles, too, even when he was in constant
employment. Organizations like the BBC, the famous opera
houses and theatrical managements seldom pay on delivery,
and he often waited weeks or months for his cheque. I recall
that once, exasperated beyond the limit of his limited patience,

he made himself some sandwiches and mixed gin with tonic in a bottle and set off for the offices of the theatre company that owed him thousands of pounds. He arrived there at nine-thirty in the morning and sat himself down opposite the secretary who had been assuring him for six months that the cheque was on her desk ready to be signed by her boss, who seemed to be permanently absent.

'I am going to sit here until he signs it. I've brought my food and drink. If I have to go to the lavatory, I shall do it on the carpet. That's a promise.'

The secretary made a series of frantic phone calls before she located the head of the company. She told him that things were desperate. The man appeared at noon and observed that he regarded David's behaviour as beneath contempt. He signed the cheque.

'May I use your telephone?' David enquired, with feigned politeness. 'What's the number of your bank? It would be so inconvenient if this bounced.'

David learned that there were sufficient funds in the account, while the terrified secretary and the apoplectic manager looked on. And with the words 'Quoth the raven' he left the premises.

He was not to be so belatedly fortunate with the management that staged the ill-fated musical *Barnardo*, about the Victorian philanthropist who founded the homes for orphaned children. This was a huge undertaking for David, so large in fact that he required the assistance of three friends whom he promised to pay handsomely. There was an initial payment. After weeks of day-and-night activity the costumes were finished and delivered. The show opened to blisteringly bad reviews. The management was forced into receivership. The cast refused to perform one night, and money was somehow found for them. They were the only people to be paid. David was never to receive the £10,000 owing to him. Yet he honoured the agreement with his friends, though it took months of back-breaking labour to do so.

He gave up drinking coffee in the mornings and substituted gin and tonic instead. His belly grew larger and larger. He never seemed to have a hangover. We were walking along a street in Fulham one Saturday morning in 1984 when he stopped suddenly and vomited blood. We were not far from a hospital. He was attended to immediately in Accidents and Emergencies and the bleeding was brought to a stop. He was given an anaesthetic and later that day he was transferred to the Intensive Care Unit at Westminster Hospital, which was to become, in his own words, his 'second home'. It was there that the doctor who was tending him told me, in a very loud voice that everyone in the corridor could hear, that if he didn't stop drinking alcohol he would die. He would die, the doctor added, horribly. David was embarrassed and offended by this announcement, which caused staff and patients to stare at him, but it ensured that he would be teetotal for the rest of his life.

The nurses and doctors in the Intensive Care Unit admired him for his humour, his freedom from self-pity and his refusal to turn his face to the wall. The man who had been committing suicide by stealth for years was now possessed of a ferocious will to live. He refused to believe what those who loved him knew already – that he had left it too late. Whenever the instruments of survival were removed from his neck, his arms, his chest, he was unfailingly cheerful. I sat by his bed for an entire night and when a friend came to visit him the next morning I went out to get a cup of coffee and a croissant. I returned within the hour to find him sitting up and laughing. I gazed at him in amazement and anger. He was the most carefree Lazarus that could be imagined.

I brought the puppy home in April 1985 and for almost a year he revelled in her company. 'How's Circe?' would be his first question when he saw me entering the Intensive Care Unit in the summer, autumn and winter of his unlikely *annus mirabilis*.

He was frequently tired, but the irrepressible animal, nipping at our ankles as if we were the sheep she had been trained to round up, amused and charmed him. He took Polaroid photographs of her – one, captured when she was very young, peeing on a broadsheet newspaper, fell out of a book just the other day, causing me to smile and weep. It is the earliest token of his affection for her.

One memory of his devotion to the intruder will suffice. It was a day in the late summer of 1985, and we were walking by the Thames in Chiswick in the company of two friends and their small sons, who were then five and three. We decided to cross Hammersmith Bridge and stroll along the towpath on the other side. We were halfway across when Circe slipped from her lead and dashed into the traffic. I froze with terror. The ever-practical David, despite his illness, leapt after her, catching her by the scruff of the neck and slapping her until she yelped. She was put back on the lead, and the collar was tightened in order to prevent another attempted escape.

'You bloody fool,' he yelled at me. And then he expressed thanks to the driver of the car that had come to a swift halt in front of the man and the dog.

At six o'clock on the morning of 15 March 1986, I awoke to

find him dressed and packed. He'd had an attack in the night, had phoned the Intensive Care Unit and ordered a minicab, which drew up outside five minutes later.

We kissed goodbye.

'I don't want to come back this time.' He spoke without emotion. His last words were: 'Look after Circe.'

Disque Bleu

The Arab offered me a cigarette. 'Smoke?' he asked. I shook my head, and smiled to express my gratitude. He had a little boy with him, whose hair he ruffled. 'Girl' was his next word, followed a minute or so later by 'new', then 'baby'. I indicated with a nod what he was attempting to tell me. He had come to register the birth of his daughter. He had already guessed that I was there to record someone's death. My face had told him as much. He had recognized grief, and acknowledged it with a small gesture of kindness – the only one available to him in the curious circumstances.

That brief meeting took place on the afternoon of 27 March 1986, in a waiting room in the Westminster Council House. I remember how the Arab tried to contain his happiness by adopting a serious expression whenever our eyes met. I was touched, and slightly amused, by the way in which he manoeuvred the change from obvious delight to awkward sympathy. I desperately wanted to tell him not to bother; that the offer of the rather foul-smelling cigarette had been enough. My name was called first, and before I left I muttered words I thought he might know: 'Thanks,' I said, and, 'Congratulations'.

'Not *quite* the youngest this week,' the woman who took the death certificate from me remarked. 'There was one yesterday who was only forty-six.' She was stating a matter of fact. I watched her as she read the slip of paper. 'It isn't for me to ask you why,' she observed, writing 'cirrhosis of the liver' alongside David's name in the large ledger on the table between us. 'Guilt,' I ventured, without explanation. 'I think it was guilt.' I sat in silence until she finished. When I rose to leave, she advised me to enjoy the rest of my life. Her tone was almost brusque. 'Yes,' I heard myself answer.

As soon as I got home, I took Circe for a brief walk and then telephoned the undertaker nearest to the hospital in which David had died. 'It's Easter in a few days' time,' said the man I talked to. 'We're pretty heavily booked.' Could he have my number? He would see what he could do. He rang back the following morning. 'You're in luck, Mr Bailey,' the fruity voice announced. 'There's been a last-minute cancellation.' I nearly laughed, but managed to say something absurd, like 'Good' instead.

The owner of the fruity voice had a rubicund face to match. 'I'm a failed actor,' he informed me. I had noticed a copy of the *Stage* on his desk. 'You need to be a bit of a thespian in this job.' I accepted his invitation to 'take a pew'. 'Shall we run through your requirements?' We began with the most basic. Was it to be a burial or a cremation? On hearing it was the latter, he recommended Mortlake for its 'atmosphere'. I replied that Mortlake was perfectly suitable. What kind of coffin did I prefer – plain wood, or walnut perhaps, or even mahogany? 'Plain wood,' I answered. 'Very practical, Mr Bailey. Very sensible. It's going to be burnt, after all.' He cleared his throat and inquired if my 'late companion' was religious. He was a lapsed Catholic, I told him. 'We have plenty of those,' he said, and chuckled. 'In that case, will you be requiring a clergyman or priest?' We were virtually soulmates by now. 'Good God, no,' I said. 'Very sensible, yet again. You've saved yourself a hundred and twenty pounds.'

A secular service presented no problems, he assured me. 'I'm afraid it's restricted to thirty minutes maximum,' he added. He suggested that a rehearsal might be in order, given that I intended to read some Jane Austen, play a couple of tapes of Mozart arias, and have a friend address the mourners. I'd already revealed that I'd once been an actor. 'Timing's of the essence, Mr Bailey.'

Mr Bailey heeded his advice, and rehearsed the readings from *Pride and Prejudice* and *Persuasion* with only Circe to hear them. The funeral director made sure that the first act trio from *Così fan tutte* and 'Porgi amor' from *Figaro* came in and out on cue, and the publisher who praised David did so with feeling and wit and brevity. My red-faced adviser had proposed that everyone should depart in advance of the coffin's disappearance. 'Such an upsetting moment. Sliding away behind those curtains. Much too *final*.'

After the service, which had been a celebratory affair, my unlikely soulmate took me aside and confessed that the publisher's speech had moved him deeply. 'I have to tell you, Mr Bailey, that I too am gay,' he said in a near-whisper, and then wagged an admonitory finger: 'Not a word to the staff.' He was ashamed to be dishonest – but, well, there it was. His guarded confession was the more poignant because I was certain that the people who worked with him were fully aware that he was homosexual. I found, and still find, his innocence beguiling, and his unnecessary discretion both comic and sad.

'The ashes are in my office, safe and sound,' he phoned to say. 'Come along when you're ready.' It was weeks, months, before I was ready. He was as cheerful as ever on the day I called to collect the urn that contained them. He poured me a sherry. 'Do you remember the joke I made, Mr Bailey?' He'd made so many jokes, I wasn't certain which particular one he had in mind. 'The cancellation joke,' he reminded me. He proceeded to quote himself, in a fruitier voice than his customarily fruity one: '"You're in luck, Mr Bailey. There's been a last-minute cancellation".' Of course I remembered it. 'I was testing you,' he confided. 'I try it on all my clients. You hesitated, and I knew you wanted to laugh. If you'd reacted differently, I'd have treated you more *solemnly*.' I said I was glad he hadn't; that his jokes, his performance, had been a comfort. I couldn't imagine him being solemn. 'It's well within my range, solemnity,' he intoned.

I had a novel to finish and, in the immediate period after David's death, I wrote the closing fifty pages of *Gabriel's Lament* in a kind of haze, with Circe often curled about my feet.

The gently courteous Arab, the brisk registrar of births and deaths, the histrionic funeral director will continue to be vivid presences in my life. Each of them was distinctly thoughtful, distinctly solicitous.

'Your late companion was fortunate in his friends,' said my

soulmate when I went to collect the ashes. 'A most impressive turnout. He must have been a popular chap.'

'He was.'

'Unlike some I could tell you about.'

He told me about a rich old man who had written 'reams and reams of dire epic verse'. The 'poet' had arranged that his service should run for an hour and a half – the time it took the funeral director to read his masterpiece aloud: 'An appalling piece of doggerel, Mr Bailey. I performed it for what it was worth, which – alas – wasn't much.'

The chapel at Mortlake was filled to capacity with the old man's relatives, who listened to the endless doggerel with feigned interest. Some gave up the effort, and fell asleep. 'There was a woman in the front row *snoring*.' They were there in anticipation of the versifier's will, which was read the same day.

'Theirs was a wasted journey, Mr Bailey. Not a sausage did he leave them. Not a single solitary *sausage*. Everything was left to charity.' He laughed. 'Let's toast the Keats that never was with another sherry.'

Tour de Powys

Circe and I spent the long Easter weekend after David's death on my agent's farm in Powys, near the Welsh border. The dog was at her happiest as she scampered across the fields at daybreak. I strolled behind her. The ball was forgotten. There were too many interesting smells to sniff out, and so much unknown territory to explore. She often turned and glanced at me impatiently, as if to accuse her sluggish master of being unadventurous. I had the impending funeral on my mind, and the question of what food I should prepare for the mourners. Grief, for the moment, was almost of secondary importance.

Circe chose to imagine that I and my closest friends could be rounded up like sheep. Human ankles were for nipping at. On that first excursion into the countryside, there were real sheep on the horizon, bleating at the approach of a stranger and his dog. To my relief, Circe went nowhere near them. She hurried on, indifferent to their presence and their noise. They were no concern of hers.

On one of those Easter mornings, I saw a man with a shotgun in the immediate distance. He was staring at Circe with keen interest. I realized that he was wondering if she was a fox, so I began to run, yelling her name. He, in turn, must have comprehended that I wasn't some eccentric with a feral pet and greeted me with an abrupt time of day.

A year later, we stayed with Deborah, her husband Michael and their infant daughter, Jessica, again. On a fine spring afternoon three of us were sitting in front of the farmhouse, enjoying a drink, when Circe suddenly became agitated, her ears cocked, her tail wagging frantically. Within seconds, she darted off down the track that leads to the farm and was soon on the main road. We now caught sight of what she had seen – a team of cyclists, professionals to judge by their high-speed bicycles and the outfits they were wearing, who were facing the challenge of the steep hill ahead. Circe joined them in that endeavour.

Fearing for her safety, Michael and I gave chase in the car. The cyclists had no intention of stopping, and neither had Circe. She ran alongside them, matching their speed. They were breathless when they attained the peak of the hill, getting off their bikes and collapsing in a smiling heap on the grass verge. And Circe, an honoured addition to the team, fell at their feet, gasping like them and in a similar state of exhaustion.

'That's some animal you've got there,' one of the cyclists managed to say.

'Yes,' I answered politely, though I was seething with fury about the silly and dangerous game they had allowed her to play.

They stroked and patted her upturned belly and told her what a clever girl she was.

She became less boisterous as she got older. She was fifteen when, to my horror and amazement, she reverted to the worrying habit of her giddy youth. We were coming to the end of the morning run in Ravenscourt Park. I saw a cyclist in nearby Paddenswick Road, and so did she. Off she sped, old as she was, as she'd sped long ago, and my heart beat faster at the thought of her being run over. But she and I were lucky, for another dog owner – a woman of few words – was standing at the pedestrian crossing with her two charges. She grabbed hold of Circe with her free left hand and chided her for her bad behaviour. I thanked the woman and apologized for my dog's recklessness.

That was Circe's final brush with death. Many more cyclists were to come into her line of vision, but she merely barked at them now. I recalled that afternoon in 1987, and the chase up the hill, and her moments of glory when she reached the peak. Those cyclists had complimented her on her quickness and cleverness, and she had basked in their sincere appreciation, while I could only bless the fates for sparing her once again.

Trial by Jury

In July 1986 I was summoned to do jury service at Acton Crown Court. I took Circe to the park as soon as it opened, dragged her home a little earlier than usual and then set off to be a responsible citizen. During that happy week I sat in on two extraordinary trials, both of which I remember keenly.

The first involved a personable young black man who was stopped for speeding in Oxford Street. When questioned by the two policemen who brought him to a halt, he explained that he taught baseball at a college of further education and that he was late for class. The constables insisted that he open the boot of his car. He did so, and a baseball bat was revealed. Although he had already told them the nature of his work, one of the policemen asked him what he used the bat for. He was astonished, and in his astonishment risked a joke. 'For hitting people like you,' he replied with a smile. He was instantly arrested and later charged with being in possession of a dangerous weapon.

The defendant smiled throughout his day-long trial. The policemen appeared, separately, in the witness box. Each said that the other had ordered the man to open the boot, and each announced that he had asked the question that led to the man's arrest.

The principal of the college spoke glowingly of the teacher's achievements. His sunny disposition made him immensely popular with the students. He could never resist a joke, and that was the reason he was in court. If he had a failing, it was his inability to curb his tongue.

We, the jury, adjourned to deliberate. Eleven of us, including an eloquently persuasive Indian, agreed that the case was farcical. There was a solitary dissident – a grey-faced woman who kept insisting that if you couldn't trust the police you couldn't trust anyone. The fact that the policemen had only brought the young man to trial with their own promotion in mind had to be spelt out to her for a wearying hour or so. If he'd been white, he would have been fined for speeding, his excuse would have been believed, and the boot never opened.

'You have to have faith in the police,' she reiterated. 'I was brought up to have faith in the police.'

On this particular occasion, the Indian observed sweetly, her faith was misplaced. Hadn't she noticed that the men's statements differed? The defence counsel had seized on this obvious truth. We had to bring in a unanimous verdict.

The woman, complaining that she wasn't pleased with what she was doing, finally relented. I was elected to speak for my fellow jurors.

The judge congratulated us on our decision. He accused the police of wasting the court's time and of humiliating a patently innocent man. He ended by advising the teacher of baseball to refrain from making a joke if he was ever apprehended again. The teacher's smile was now fulsome.

The second trial I attended was brief and bizarre. The defendant was an elegantly dressed man in his thirties who was arrested on his return to England from America, where he had been working for five years. His case was therefore history. The charge against him was that he and another man had committed an act of gross indecency in the cemetery adjoining Brompton Oratory at three in the morning. It was alleged that he and his partner had indulged in mutual masturbation whilst seated on a tomb. A titter ran through the court when the prosecuting counsel declared that the men had caused grave offence to the public. The man in the dock allowed himself the trace of a smile.

Before our deliberations were over – the Indian wondering precisely who was being offended at three in the morning – we were instructed to return to the courtroom. The man had been advised to plead guilty, as the other man in the case had done, and was consequently fined £50 and cautioned. I thought of the 'law's delay' and the 'insolence of office' on my way home to Circe, who would be desperate for exercise.

I arrived at Acton Crown Court the following Monday, happily anticipating another week of intense human interest. I was to be disappointed. A major trial was about to begin, the defendants were four black men who were charged with drug-dealing, affray, and grievous bodily harm, as I later discovered. I was among the eighteen who were called into court for the selection of a jury. I can't recall why, but on that morning I was carrying a copy of the *Daily Telegraph*, a paper I have written for but seldom read. A solicitor representing the four advised his clients to reject me on the grounds that a *Telegraph* reader would not be sympathetic to their cause; would be, indeed, downright hostile. I was released from jury service at lunchtime.

The baseball coach and the man on the tomb causing grave offence to an insomniac public anxious to visit cemeteries while the rest of the populace was sleeping – I think of them both with distant affection, and of how they reminded me of life's petty misfortunes; of the traps awaiting those of us who can neither curb our tongues nor suppress our sudden, inflammatory desires.

Jam Today

The kitchen was mine at last, now that David's brilliant reign of culinary tyranny was over. We had moved it to the top floor of the house some years earlier, revelling in its spaciousness and the light that flooded in on all but the darkest winter days. David had bought a large gas cooker that resembled in design a small cinema organ. (I half-expected music, rather than gas, to come out of it when the switches were turned on.) It had two temperamental doors that swung open whenever the oven reached a certain level of heat. The doors were 'fixed' by a succession of repairmen, who unscrewed them, refitted them, realigned them and even, on one occasion, replaced them. Yet their handiwork was to no permanent avail, since there would continue to be a terrible moment when the doors, having behaved themselves for weeks, decided not to stay closed. David would shout and curse, and an old chair would have to be jammed against the doors, and Circe would let out a single bark and dart downstairs, not wanting to be involved in the drama.

High drama was an essential feature of David's cooking. Tension mounted as soon as he approached the stove. Nothing less than complete perfection satisfied him. The recipes that most appealed to him were elaborate, requiring enormous reserves of patience to prepare, and there were times – not too many – when his patience was tried to breaking-point. To stay calm, he often cooked to the accompaniment of *The*

Marriage of Figaro, to Handel's *Messiah* and to Pergolesi's *Stabat Mater*. Silence was not to be countenanced, except when he was studying a new, and ever more complicated, dish. In his final months, he created meals for rich customers who sent couriers to collect them. And sometimes, if he was well enough, he went to their houses and businesses to oversee the preparation of the central masterpiece on cookers blessed with unproblematic doors.

The kitchen became a quiet place in the spring of 1986. My book was finished and already in proof. I was a cook again, and pleased that I could entertain friends with dishes I hadn't made in an eternity. I discovered recipes that excited me in books by Claudia Roden, Alice Waters and the refreshingly eccentric Patience Gray, whose *Honey from a Weed* can also be read for its insights into literature, painting and sculpture. David had only ever allowed me to make shepherd's pie, the 'comfort food' he liked best, but now – grieving and lonely – I was free to prepare whatever I desired. The Mexican Garlic Soup in Alice Waters's *Chez Panisse Menu Cookbook*; the Spicy Prawns in Claudia Roden's *A New Book of Middle Eastern Food*, and the wild concoction of aubergines, onions, tomatoes and herbs Patience Gray chanced upon in a Greek village – these became, and still are, favourites with my cherished friends. They would be joined by the glorious Russian Raspberry Tart from Margaret Costa's excellent *Four Seasons Cookery Book*.

I had time to fill, or perhaps kill, and Circe helped me fill it. Each morning she would propel me to the park, where I frequently had to throw the ball for as much as two hours. She had the sheepdog's habit of running in a circle, cleverly retrieving the ball from unexpected angles, catching it between her teeth while still in motion. Passers-by would stop to admire and applaud.

Other dogs achieved exhaustion fairly rapidly, but not Circe. I marvelled at, and was sometimes exasperated by, her unflagging liveliness. She seemed to be willing herself not to get tired. It was only when she flopped on to the grass, panting heavily, that I knew she was ready to go home. Or was she? As soon as we were outside the park she began to draw back on the lead. The beast who had towed me earlier now had to be dragged homewards. This was a double spectacle the neighbours found diverting – that of a man being pulled along the street by an eager dog, and of the same man trying to coax the same, suddenly reluctant, dog into following him.

I was in a state of blank despair on the afternoon I decided to occupy myself by making jam. I went out and bought plums, raisins, blanched almonds and a bottle of dark rum. I cut the plums into halves, and put the stones in a small saucepan, covering them with half-a-pint of water. I boiled the stones for ten minutes, and drained the liquid through a sieve. This I poured over the plums and raisins I had placed in a larger pan. I let the mixture simmer over a low heat. When the fruit had softened, I took the pan off the gas and added the requisite amount of sugar, which I stirred in until it was completely dissolved. I put the pan back on the ring and watched it carefully, stirring at intervals to prevent the jam thickening too quickly or getting burnt. Concentration, of a satisfyingly mindless kind, was necessary. I concentrated on the task I had chosen. I removed the pan from the heat and threw in the finely chopped almonds and four tablespoons of rum. More stirring was needed, and then the glistening jam was ready for the pots I had previously sterilized. I tasted it when it had cooled a little, and realized I was in possession of a new, unanticipated talent. To stave off depression, or to lighten it at least, I had only to go to the stove and perfect my skills as a jam-maker.

And that's what I did, and am still doing. I like making jams, jellies and chutneys when the fruit is in season, though there are some you can rustle up at any time in the year – dried apricot, for instance, and the exotic Creole jam, composed of bananas, the juice and zest of two or three limes, a spoonful of cinnamon and a generous measure of rum. The friends and acquaintances who enjoy this tend to be exotic themselves – given to owning parrots or mynah birds, or communing with the Beyond via a number of middle-aged women with suburban addresses that boast names – 'Rest-a-While', 'Magnolia Lodge' – instead of numbers.

Once a year, and that once is enough, a friend brings me crab apples and medlars from her garden. The patience called upon to convert these inedible fruits into appetizing jellies is of the superhuman kind, what with straining the liquid through muslin and ensuring that not one precious drop – and every drop *is* precious – is wasted.

I seldom eat my own jam, preferring to give it away to the

appreciative and to those I wish to thank for acts of kindness. Making it properly affords me enough satisfaction. 'Sweet are the uses of adversity' – it's strange to look back on that summer afternoon when I found a means to keep grief at bay for an hour or so.

Clearance

Edie stood in state in the front room for months after David's death. Circe, waking from a long sleep, would bark at her, hoping perhaps for some response from the curious individual with no arms, legs or head. Edie's sizeable bosom did not heave at the sound. She was fixed to her spot, in the bay of the window.

Edie was David's tailor's dummy. Dresses worn by many of the greatest opera singers of the second half of the twentieth century had been put together piece by piece on Edie's immobile frame. The corset that had given Montserrat Caballé the unexpected bonus of a waist had been moulded and built on Edie.

How did she come to be called Edie? In 1961, three years before meeting David, I was in the company of the then Shakespeare Memorial Theatre at Stratford-upon-Avon playing the smallest of small parts, carrying spears and understudying robustly healthy actors. In *Richard III*, in which I appeared as Lovel, Eric Porter played Buckingham with guileful authority. Each night in the wings, shortly before his first entrance, he would hitch up his robe and say something outrageous to make us all laugh. A favourite, much-repeated *cri de coeur* that Eric loved to deliver was the one expressed by a distraught brothel keeper alerting her maid-of-all-work to the prospect of custom: 'Not a pisspot emptied, not an armpit washed, and the street full of Spanish sailors. Edie!' Eric would lower his robe and march on to the stage with a retinue of nobles behind him struggling desperately to keep their faces straight.

So the overwoked 'Edie', emptying the pots and supervising the scrubbing of armpits, gave her oft-shrieked name to the dummy. The inanimate Edie was photographed beside me in the autumn of 1986 for a magazine article to coincide with the publication of my novel *Gabriel's Lament*. The young photographer, Chris, was amused by her presence in an otherwise conventionally furnished room. The photograph was shown in an exhibition at the National Portrait Gallery after Chris's death on the *Marchioness*, the pleasure boat that sank in the Thames on 20 August 1989.

Edie was the last of David's possessions to go. Friends were grateful to receive his sewing machine, the corsets and bodices and an array of leftover fabrics. These were a pleasure to dispense. Only his clothes remained in the wardrobe. For a while I was unable even to touch them.

Then, one morning, I returned from the park with the dog, and in an automatic daze I filled bags with shirts, jackets, sweaters, trousers, shoes. I carried them to the nearest charity shop, and on reaching home I tore up all the remaining pictures of him. I was staggered at the ease with which I performed what seemed like an act of ruthlessness. I wanted some part of our past to be obliterated.

Edie is now resident in Bloomsbury, where her chest and waist are still giving service. What I have of David, apart from his undying presence, is an exquisite gold neck chain and the Swiss watch he bought for me when he was flush. Daily reminders; lasting gifts.

The Woman in Whites and the Man with a Mission

I first noticed the would-be tennis player more than twenty years ago, when the last bloom of youth was beginning to fade from both our faces. She was always immaculately turned out in pristine, pleated, white shorts and a crisply ironed white blouse. Her white socks and running shoes were equally clean, with no traces of turf on them. She carried a racquet, a string bag containing tennis balls, and an elegant leather handbag. She sometimes wore a pink bow in her neat blonde hair.

She had much to say to herself, of an earnest nature, to judge by the sharpness of her tone and the furrows on her forehead. I often wondered if she had two voices at her command – her own, and that of an unseen partner or contestant. Was this person on the other side of the net, perhaps, or playing alongside her in doubles? Here was a game that seemed to be in perpetual progress, with no foreseeable ending. Or so I fancied, imagining that a real match on a real court had been halted, and could only be resumed, again and again, in her mind. Her outfit might be the equivalent of Miss Havisham's wedding dress, and her tennis match that famously cancelled marriage ceremony, with its uneaten cake, its absent groom.

It was with the arrival of Circe that I came to realize that the woman, when kitted out for tennis, saw nothing beyond her immediate vision of the interrupted game. She was oblivious to the dog's bark of welcome, and strode on, racquet at the ready, muttering darkly in one of her voices. Circe never failed to acknowledge her, and the woman never stopped to stroke, or talk to, the animal whose approval she had gained. How had she gained it? That was another mystery, and not open to supposition, like the aborted singles or doubles. Circe wanted to be her friend, as she didn't want be be the friend of other men and women whose shows of affection she either ignored or rebuffed. And then, one day, the mystery was instantly solved. It wasn't the woman's friendship Circe craved, it was the tantalizing tennis balls in the string bag. I had been a blind fool, not to have seen what was obvious.

In the last year or so of Circe's life, I had to change my mind. The woman wore different whites now – white skirt, white blouse, white stockings, white raincoat. It could be that the match had been won in her head, or finally abandoned, for she no longer carried the racquet and the string bag. She was still engaged in frantic conversation with herself, however, and still heedless of Circe's genial overtures. The dog still wished to be friends.

Circe had no trouble attracting Mick's attention. 'She's a pretty thing,' he would say. Mick, like the one-time tennis fan, is Irish, and like her he has been institutionalized. In common with many Irish people in the district, he had been born and raised on a farm, and was used to the company of sheepdogs. He grinned at the eager Circe and patted her gently.

Mick was once prone to violent fits, and was often taken away and placed in protective care for months at a stretch. That was years ago. For the last decade he has been a model of amiability, because he is happy in his chosen work. He is not paid for it, though courteous passers-by stop and thank him for picking up the litter the unsociable have discarded.

Mick can be seen every day of the year at the corner of the road by Starch Green, placing empty packets, tissues, cigarette ends, leaves – and even dog turds, which he wraps in paper – in the bins the sane inhabitants of Hammersmith have overlooked. Mick performs this task with a zeal that deserves to be called missionary, for there is a light in his eyes as he goes up and down, to and fro, keeping his half-mile clean. He usually has a word to say about the weather, and if he talks to himself it is to chide the men and women – and children, mostly – for whom he is tidying up. The shopkeepers and the fellow residents of the council estate where he lives regard him fondly, as indeed they should. He is providing them with a service, after all, in his smiling fashion.

Geoffrey's Socks

Circe was as much in need of exercise at home as she was within the relatively wide open spaces of the park. Throwing a ball for her was neither sensible nor feasible because there were too many objects in the house that could be easily broken. What else was there to hurl down the stairwell? Socks, old socks, was the answer.

The discarded socks were David's and mine. They were made of cotton or light wool, and therefore not resistant to Circe's strong teeth. Her saliva soon rendered them offensive to the touch. Jane Grigson was sitting with me in the kitchen on a fine summer evening a few weeks after David's death, watching me throw a rolled-up sock over the banister for the ever-scuttling dog. Circe, retrieving it, dropped the soggy toy at Jane's feet with an abrupt bark that indicated it was her, Jane's, turn. Jane picked it up, pulled a face registering mild disgust, and said, 'Next time I come, I'll bring you some socks that won't end up like this.' She slung the sock away from her, and it was quickly brought back, in an even soggier state.

Jane kept her promise. She arrived bearing gifts, as was her generous custom – Yarg, a delicious new cheese from Cornwall; green figs, just about to ripen; a bottle of balsamic vinegar. And then she produced the treat for Circe, who was smiling at her, tail wagging. From out of her bag came two pairs of her husband's socks, one red, one blue. They were sturdy, countryman's socks, of the kind that go with stout shoes or boots. They had been lovingly darned, I saw. It would take an excess of salivating to make them limp.

'There are more where those came from.'

And there were. Geoffrey Grigson's chilblain-proof socks became Circe's household toys. They were a mouthful for her. Guests were invited to share in her untiring fun. Some visitors, it has to be noted, were happier with this diversion than others. Circe was perplexed when the proffered sock was ignored, her bewilderment giving way to irritation. She barked and barked, and had to be banished from the kitchen with a stern 'Enough'. I would put the sock out of sight and out of reach and she would sulk in the front room until it was time to play again.

In the summer of 1975, I wrote a review for the *New Statesman* of a book by Geoffrey Grigson called *Britain Observed*. The literary editor allotted me 1,200 words, which meant that I had the long-coveted opportunity of being able to put his career into some kind of balanced perspective. It was an honour and duty to do so since Geoffrey had the reputation then – as, alas, he has now – of being little more than a scurrilous and intemperate critic. People remembered his dislike and disapproval of Edith Sitwell, Dylan Thomas and a host of tin-eared academics, whilst forgetting or overlooking the substantial fact that in his thirties and forties he 'rescued' those extraordinary English geniuses John Clare, Samuel Palmer, William Barnes and George Crabbe from near-oblivion. He published the early poems of W. H. Auden in his pioneering magazine *New Verse*, and discovered the very young Gavin Ewart, whose 'Phallus in Wonderland' and 'Miss Twye' he was delighted to print. *Britain Observed* proved ideal as a vehicle for expressing my considered opinion that Geoffrey Grigson, with whom I was unacquainted, is essentially a celebrator, for in its pages he praises not only Cézanne and Pissarro – 'the greatest and humblest of landscape painters' – but such modest, and genuine, talents as Walter Greaves, who painted views of the Thames at Chelsea, the tragic William James Blacklock, dead at forty-two, whose beautiful *Catbells and Causey Pike* is reproduced, and Wenceslas Hollar, represented by his marvellous etching of the East Side of London in 1647, simple in essence yet vividly suggestive of overcrowded city life. The book is subtitled *The Landscape Through Artists' Eyes*, and it's typical of Grigson's eclecticism and respect for the undervalued that of those sixty-odd artists a good third of them are still unknown to the public at large.

The received, or safe, opinion was anathema to him. He was always his own man with his own mind. It seemed appropriate that I should come to praise him in the *New Statesman*, because it was in that educative journal that I first encountered his criticism, along with that of V. S. Pritchett and D. J. Enright, in the late 1950s. The back half of the *Statesman* was required reading in the 1960s, when Grigson was a regular reviewer. He flourished under the editorship of

Karl Miller, just as he had flourished under that of J. R. Ackerley on the *Listener* – both men earning his lasting regard for allowing him to write 'without fear or favour' (the words are Ackerley's.) It was from those idiosyncratic reviews – elegantly phrased and pithily argued – that I learned about Edwin Arlington Robinson's exquisite poems of everyday madness and despair in small-town America and the *Icelandic Journals* of William Morris, which makes even the bleakest landscape interesting. Grigson was one of my educators, at a time in my life when I was attempting to free myself of the burden of wanting to succeed as a classical actor. I read his criticism, and then the works he praised. And every so often, I glanced at those books that he alone held up to ridicule, such as Iris Murdoch's novel *The Unicorn*, in which characters 'cast roguish glances' at each other, 'converse' rather than talk, and say things like 'I'll be bound!' and 'Effingham, she is destroyed'. His review of the inescapable Anthony Burgess's collection *Urgent Copy: Literary Studies* caused its author lasting resentment. Grigson began his accurate and funny piece by quoting Burgess to the effect that writing books 'engenders tobacco addiction, an over-reliance on caffeine and dexedrine, piles, dyspepsia, chronic anxiety, sexual impotence'. Grigson's comment on this boast in disguise was, simply, 'Not in everyone. And not all of them, I hope, in Mr Burgess.'

Grigson pounced on the vainglorious observation 'I was in Russia when Ernest Hemingway died' and went on:

Well, if he was, the fact doesn't in any real way affect what little Mr Burgess goes on to tell us about the art of Hemingway. He might as well have begun that he was paying his rates at the council offices or catching crayfish at Piddletrenthide or declaiming Yeats over

pints of Guinness above the waves of the Bournemouth sewage
outfall, when Hemingway died. In short I can never quite believe
Mr Burgess, in this book (I know nothing of his novels). 'Old yokels
in Adderbury, my former Oxfordshire home, talk of the Earl of
Rochester as though he only died yesterday.' Really? And as they
talk of him in their smock-frocks do they quote with an Oxfordshire
– not Oxford – accent 'Drudging in fair Aurelia's womb' or 'Ancient
Person of my Heart'?

That was written in 1968. Burgess was still smarting from it
fourteen years later. In his novel *The End of the World News*,
published in 1982, Burgess has a character enter a saloon
somewhere in the Midwest of America. There is a poster on the
wall bearing the message beneath a mugshot: WANTED FOR
MURDER: DANGEROUS GEOFF GRIGSON. I phoned Geoffrey,
now a dear friend, soon after reading that scene. He laughed
heartily at the 'old bugger's cheek'. He thought it a good joke.

Burgess wasn't content with that conceit. In review after
review – spanning two decades – he found an excuse, often a
very feeble one, to sneak in a reference to his self-appointed
enemy. These gratuitous asides must have mystified the average reader, who would have been unaware of the original
cause of Burgess's spleen. They certainly bemused his widow,
who regarded them as evidence of pettiness and meanness
of spirit. Burgess's last swipe at Geoffrey, to my knowledge,
appeared in the *Observer* in March 1990, while Jane lay in a coma,
dying. She would have laughed it off, had she been able to.

Reviewing *Britain Observed*, I concentrated on Grigson the
celebrator, the man who judged each individual work – poem
or painting – on its own merit. Reputation meant nothing to
him. He had seen reputations come and go. What was import-

ant to him was freshness of vision, as exemplified by those artists who capture the passing moment, in whatever form, and thus ensure that it will last for ever.

Grigson read my article, and some weeks later I was invited to a contributors' party at the *New Statesman*'s offices in Great Turnstile in the City. I declined. Then, on the day before the party, I received a call from the literary editor with the message that both the Grigsons, husband and wife, wished to meet me. So I went along, and a friendship developed on the instant. It was as warmly simple as that. Geoffrey was to live another ten years, the much-younger Jane another fifteen. Every visit to Broad Town in Wiltshire, to the old farmhouse in which they lived, was a magical occasion, particularly in summer when we sat in the garden eating the food Jane had prepared with such loving attentiveness. And 'loving' is the apt word to account for their marriage – his third, her first and last – for they quite simply glowed in each other's company.

Geoffrey called Jane his 'Dutch interior', and indeed she would have looked – with her generous figure and ruddy complexion – perfectly at home in a painting by Pieter de Hooch or Rembrandt, or in Vermeer's *A Maid Asleep* in the Metropolitan Museum in New York. In Geoffrey she had found the 'older man of her dreams', as the curator and art critic Bryan Robertson, with whom she worked in a Cambridge gallery in the 1950s, shrewdly noted. Jane's arrival in Geoffrey's life was one of those everyday miracles that only seem to happen in the pages of sloppy romantic novels, with Mr and Miss Right meeting by chance and declaring undying love in the final chapter. Even so, those chance meetings and heartfelt declarations, for all that they come coated in linguistic glucose, do occur in the real, messy world most of us inhabit.

And so it was with Jane and Geoffrey, in their fashion. Jane had admired Geoffrey's writing from her student days – his pioneering *Samuel Palmer: The Visionary Years* of 1947; his remarkable autobiography *The Crest on the Silver*, as well as his criticism – and was determined to meet him someday, somehow. When they did meet, at an exhibition in London, it was a blessing for both of them. Jane was a natural peacemaker, exuding warmth and a disinterested understanding of other people's problems, and she brought peace to the unhappy Grigson household, as the son and daughters of his first two marriages acknowledged at Jane's funeral.

Jane became Geoffrey's happy amanuensis, typing his books and articles and poems. She had no idea, then, of becoming a writer herself, though she had already published a translation of Beccaria's classic treatise *On Crime and Punishments*, for which she received the John Florio Prize. Her distinguished career, as the true successor to Elizabeth David, whom she admired and subsequently befriended, began in an unusual way. For several weeks each year the Grigsons and their daughter, Sophie, lived in a cave-house in Trôo, in the Bas-Vendômois region of France. One of their cave-dwelling neighbours was Adey Horton, whose book *Child Jesus* had been praised by Kenneth Clark. Horton, a notorious non-deliverer of promised typescripts, had been commissioned by the publisher Michael Joseph to write a cookbook on *charcuterie* and pork cookery in general. When Jane met him, he had hardly begun work on it, despite many reminders by letter and telephone from his editor in London. He invited Jane to be his researcher and secretary. Jane accepted, and worked so diligently and thoroughly and produced such a number of detailed notes for Horton to consult that he suggested she finish the book instead. She took on the challenge with some trepidation. *Charcuterie and French Pork Cookery* appeared in 1967 and was instantly acclaimed, not least by Elizabeth David, who saluted its originality.

The critical success of that first book, which might never have been written if Adey Horton had been more conscientious, encouraged Jane to think ahead and start a new life as a food writer. In 1968, she was offered a job on the *Observer* Colour Magazine, to which she contributed regular articles until within weeks of her death twenty-two years later. Her column was notable for its insistence that good cooking is impossible without the right, fresh ingredients. She wasn't prudish on the subject, but she did regret the vanishing of the seasons. She travelled throughout Britain and Europe in pursuit of excellence – talking to farmers, suppliers, fruit growers, butchers, fishmongers and her fellow writers. If she chanced on an interesting, and workable, recipe she always named its source, an act of literary politeness not often displayed by others. But then, Jane wasn't in competition with anyone. 'I think food, its quality, its origins, its preparation, is something to be studied and thought about in the same way as any other aspect of human existence,' she declares in the Introduction to *Good Things*, which was published in 1971 and consolidated her ever-rising reputation. The notion is so sensible, so basic, one might say, that it seems amazing now that she felt the need to express it. Were she alive today, she would be insisting that it cannot be repeated often enough.

'Oh, sod it all': I first heard Jane utter that mild obscenity not long after Geoffrey's death in November 1985. She was desolate with grief, and only kept on working out of a sense of duty and responsibility. In his last weeks, Geoffrey was attended to by a professional nurse, whom he shouted at one day in his frustration. He hated being old and hated the idea of dying even more. The nurse answered him back, telling him what a rude and ungrateful so-and-so he was. He was won over instantly, to such an extent that Jane accused him of falling in love with her. Jane and the nurse accompanied him on his final outing to a local church, to listen to a recital of Haydn piano sonatas. Geoffrey wasn't especially musical, but he adored Haydn's warm-heartedness and mischief.

There were generous tributes to Geoffrey in the press, the most touching by the poet Peter Reading in *The Times Literary Supplement*:

I read him on Ben Nicholson and a painter I'd hitherto regarded as a clumsy eccentric – Samuel Palmer (whose pictures have seemed magical to me ever since). I was first and permanently attracted to the poems of William Barnes by Grigson's enthusiastic commentary on them. His topographical and historical guides had the same quality of pointing out something good one had somehow missed. His accounts of flora and fauna were knowledgeable and not poetically twee. His reviews amused me greatly; exposing humbuggery, spotting talent, valuing sense, zapping bunkum. They were healthy, good fun to read (though the dissected probably didn't relish them), and the attendant whines of 'cruelty' from the anti-vivisection lot were entertaining. In this desultory way many of us learned from Grigson.

The cries of 'cruelty' can still be heard, albeit faintly. He merits a couple of snotty references from Ian Hamilton in the posthumously published *Against Oblivion*, and is glibly and brusquely dismissed as 'that notorious scourge' by Selina Hastings in her biography of Rosamond Lehmann. The 'scourge' had the temerity to question the poetic talent of Cecil Day-Lewis, and to find it severely wanting. Hastings is content to record that the other critics – none of them named – disagreed.

I shall always regard my friend Geoffrey Grigson as a rescuer and discoverer. You only have to look at his anthologies to be made aware of the depth and range of his reading. He loved to grub in the Bodleian Library or the British Museum in the hope of rescuing some deserving poet (frequently the author of a solitary, deserving poem) from an ill-deserved obscurity.

In his grubbing days, he chanced on William Diaper, George Darley, and Samuel Daniel, who wrote:

> O blessed letters that combine in one
> All ages past, and make one live with all,
> By you do we confer with who are gone,
> And the dead living unto councell call:
> By you th'unborne shall have communion
> Of what we feele, and what doth us befall . . .

(Geoffrey shared Coleridge's admiration for those lines, which he loved to quote.)

For me, Grigson the enthusiast is at his most beguiling in the collection of essays *Poems and Poets*, in which he celebrates such wonders as Whitman's 'Memories of President Lincoln' and Christopher Smart's 'A Song to David' in language that is finely sensitive to what makes each poem peculiar and wonderful. An observation like the following is a world away from the criticism that is practised by his despised professors of literature. He quotes these lines from the fifty-second stanza of Smart's masterpiece:

> The grass the polyanthus cheques;
> And polished porphyry reflects,
> By the descending rill . . .

and then observes: 'Anyone who knows, by good luck, the limestone country of Raby, and of Staindrop Moor alongside, and Teesdale, will at once see the flower and the rock and the waterfall in a characteristic conjunction which Smart must have known in his County Durham days, the limestone so finely polished by centuries of the descending rill, protruding from grass chequered with the lilac umbrels, by the thousand, of the Birdseye Primrose.'

Geoffrey, whose beloved older brothers were slaughtered in the Great War, was never 'half in love with easeful death'. Extinction was the nastiest of his enemies. He loved a letter by William Cowper, written in 1790, 'after madness and pre-liminaries of vengeance and hell': 'The consideration of my short continuance here, which was once grateful to me, now fills me with regret. I would like to live and live always.'

Well, he couldn't, and nobody can. Geoffrey wrote many poems, and I fear that many of them will be forgotten. Yet there is a single poem, set down in his last years, that ought to endure in anthologies. It is short, and elegiac, and – to my ears – beautiful:

> You are young, you two, in loving:
> Why should you wonder what endearments
> Old whisper still to old in bed,
> Or what the one left will say and say,
> Aloud, when nobody overhears, to the one
> Who irremediably is dead?

Jane said, 'Oh, sod it all', and said it again and again, often with a laugh, when she was diagnosed with cervical cancer. In those final five years of our deepening friendship, we talked on the phone every evening at six, mentioning books that Geoffrey would have relished dissecting – all overpraised, most now mouldering away – and exchanging recipes. The supply of socks for Circe showed no signs of running out.

In the spring of 1989, I went with Jane on an eating tour of the Highlands of Scotland. One day we came across something memorably daft – 'daft' was one of her favourite words, which she spoke with the flat 'a' of her native Sunderland. It was a notice outside a hotel which read:

ROOMS
LESS GOOD – £12
SLIGHTLY BETTER – £16
BEST – £30

The sight of it inspired her to laughter. Her laugh was like a hoot, rising and rising in volume, and there were times when I thought it would never stop. It was a wonderful noise she made – warm, generous, unconstrained. It was the SLIGHTLY BETTER – £16 that inspired her now. I waited for Jane's hooting to cease, as curious passers-by stared in amazement. In that same small town, we went in search of a cotton shirt which I wanted to buy. The assistant in the men's clothing shop told us, 'Ye'll nae get a cotton shirt here. Try the tobacconist across the street.' The tobacconist indeed sold shirts, but not cotton ones – 'There's no call.' It was typical of Jane that she kept her laughter in check until we were outside. 'There's no call,' she repeated, and we both had hysterics for the second time.

I remember, too, that we stopped to have a picnic by Loch Ness. The monster was otherwise engaged, but an unidentifiable seabird compensated for his or her absence. It ate bread, cheese and salami on the bonnet of the car. Jane smiled, and said of the husband who had left her desolate, 'Geoffrey would have recognized the bird in an instant.' She opened a bottle of alcohol-free white wine someone had given her. 'What do you think?' she asked after we had taken a sip. Before I could reply, she said, 'It's disgusting, isn't it? Let's have the real thing.' So we did.

Later that year, I cooked lunch for Jane and Bryan Robertson, with whom she had been in love thirty years earlier in Cambridge. It was the happiest of reunions, with Bryan in unstoppable form as they exchanged memories and gossip. The pioneering curator and restorer of the Whitechapel Gallery in the 1950s and 60s – who had rescued Turner and Stubbs from disregard and neglect, and brought Jackson Pollock and Mark Rothko to the attention of the British – was hooting as heartily as Jane that day. Jane said afterwards that she had loved Bryan for his rare intelligence, for his enthusiasm, and for a quality he shared with Geoffrey – a deep, deep knowledge of books, paintings and poems that fashion had overtaken and overlooked. And when Bryan died – on 18 November 2002 – at the end of a gruesome illness, borne with much good humour and concern for his friends – I thought of Jane's high regard for him, and his glowing affection for her.

At Jane's memorial service, in the spring of 1990, I was privileged to read a poem by Geoffrey that had never been published. It was a love poem, addressed to his young bride, which Jane carried in her bag wherever she went. She needed no written confirmation of his love, which was demonstrated by look and touch, but it must have comforted her when her husband, mentor and lover was no more.

That evening, Circe played with Geoffrey's socks as usual, and for many subsequent evenings.

Minders

It was their unhealthy white fatness we noticed first. Their bellies preceded them into the park as they arrived with an assortment of dogs – a sprightly Alsatian; an artistically trimmed poodle, with a black pompom on each shaved leg; a fluffy Sealyham, and a docile Dobermann, whose interest in Circe – even when she wasn't in season – was always startlingly evident. They often held hands, like young lovers, when they weren't munching copious hamburgers.

She was small and broad. He loomed above her, his vast gut barely contained within a grubby white T-shirt. She invariably wore a tracksuit and trainers; he a black leather jacket and baggy jeans. Her hair was dank, his sleekly greased. They doted on each other and on the pets in their charge, who obeyed their every quiet command.

They were married, we learned, and had been unemployed for a long time. But now they were doing all right, walking and looking after the dogs that belonged to the rich pro-fessional people who lived in Chiswick. They loved their work and were well paid for it, in cash. We could see that the dogs liked their minders, for whom they were naturally and immediately obedient.

The couple's favourite topic of conversation, apart from the superiority of dumb animals, was crime. In actual fact, they didn't converse, but rather indulged in a dual monologue. They harangued us with their opinions on the causes of, and the cure for, murder and rape and burglary. We were subjected to the predictable views of a tabloid editorialist – hanging should be restored; a life sentence should mean a sentence for life, not ten or twenty years; thugs should receive a taste of their own punishment; black or Indian offenders should be deported. Theirs was a catalogue of unwavering imperatives.

(I suspect that a few of the more sedate dog owners secretly agreed with them, but would never have given their thoughts such crude or such public expression.)

Everyone felt relieved when the pair stopped coming to the park. Were they on holiday, perhaps? Had they found steady employment? There was no more talk of hanging and flogging and instant deportation. The everyday routine of inconsequential chat and harmless gossip was gradually re-established.

I came home one morning with the untired Circe and settled down to read the newspaper. I had a shock in store as I opened it. There, on the third page, was a photograph of the couple. Alongside it was a story that was all too depressingly familiar. It seemed they had a son, no more than a toddler, whom they had tortured, starved and beaten. His emaciated body was covered in cigarette burns. The boy had been taken from them, but had died in hospital.

On the morning they were due to stand trial, the husband threw himself from the roof of a multi-storey car park in Hammersmith. Death was instantaneous.

In the park the next day we talked in muted tones about the two dog minders. Someone had seen a picture of the child, and it had made her weep with pity and anger. Someone else wondered if the newly widowed wife had changed her mind on the subject of bringing criminals to justice.

The Mating Game

'Have you ever thought of having her mated?'

The question was put to me by an amiable stallholder in Hammersmith market – the owner of a genuine collie, not a quasi-collie like mine.

'They'd have beautiful puppies.'

I hadn't thought of having Circe mated, but now – looking at the handsome animal spread out by the fruit-and-vegetable stall – I began to consider it a possibility.

I had weathered Circe's first season by walking her very early in the morning and only taking her out when I was certain there were no dogs in the street. Even so, and in spite of my cautiousness, a determined sleuth picked up her scent and trailed it back to the house, where he let out a noise pitched between howling and barking, which Circe then started to accompany with anguished yelps. Sensing that the neighbours would soon be complaining, I filled a bucket with water and aimed it at the unprepossessing hound, who retreated, still giving voice to his frustration. He got the message that his attentions were not desired – by me, at any rate – when I doused him thoroughly with the third bucketful. He slunk off. I waited by the gate for ten minutes or more, but he did not return.

He reappeared in the morning, hopeful and silent. My presence signalled water to him, and he went away, for ever.

When Circe's second season came along, I wondered if I

was being rational. I remembered what it was like caring for and training a single puppy, and trembled at the prospect of rearing three, four, five or even six of them, beautiful or not. I had struck a bargain with the stallholder that I would keep one of the puppies and he could have the rest of the litter.

We arranged that his dog and my bitch should meet in Ravenscourt Park on Thursday afternoon. The animals duly met, with Circe making obvious overtures. The thoroughbred regarded her coquettish behaviour with disdain. He turned his back on her. She indicated with startling clarity exactly what she wanted of him, and he wandered off. He chased a squirrel, and then a pigeon, and then he lay on the grass, his eyes on his bewildered master. Circe barked and barked to no avail, for the dog was not to be roused.

The stallholder shook his head. 'It's not going to happen, is it?'

'Probably not.'

By this time a couple of other dogs, both very interested in Circe's exertions and contortions, had arrived. They were shooed off and collected by their embarrassed owners before harm was done.

So the mating game wasn't played. The stallholder and I shook hands on our failed pact and parted. I took Circe to the conservation area, where she had a cooling swim in the pond.

When she was her normal self again, I had her spayed. Yet lustful notions continued to assail her. Their object was a docile Alsatian, owned by Tony and Andy, two brothers who lived in the street. Whenever she saw him she would lie on her back and open her back legs invitingly, to the great amusement of the boys. She often tried to fellate him, and Circe and Max had to be pulled back on their leads. She remained faithful to Max until the end, rubbing her nose against his to assure him he was the only dog in the world for her.

Toby and Jumbo

There were many grand funerals in London in 1823, but one of the grandest – certainly the most unusual – was given in honour of a beggar named Billy Walters. Billy had one leg and played the violin. He was also black. It is indicative of his charm, his musical skills and his courteous demeanour, that the city streets were crammed with mourners, the overwhelming majority of whom were white.

Billy was the envy of London's regular vagrants, who were either moved on by the police or carted off to the workhouse. The more inventive and resourceful among them blackened their hands and faces and whatever parts of the body that were visible in order to attract some of his sympathetic custom. Hair must have been problematical for them, and blue or green eyes. These pretend-Negroes, it is safe to assume, lacked Billy's panache, his talent on the fiddle, as well as his missing limb. They could not match his success, hard as they tried. He was genuine, and they were fakes.

Another black mendicant who is remembered, if only faintly, in works of social history is Joseph Johnson. He was almost as celebrated in the capital as Billy, and is credited as being the first known beggar to make use of a dog. Joseph's canine accessory was called Toby and the inseparable couple stirred hearts to pity. Two pairs of dark, sad eyes proved more financially rewarding than one.

'Toby', in fact, became one of two generic names for a

begging dog. The other was 'Jumbo', which was given to plumper, healthier-looking beasts. A skinny black beggar, with his bones showing through his flesh, would keep Jumbo by his side to show his compassionate patrons that he had neglected his own welfare in his pet's interests. Apprentice beggars could choose between a Toby or a Jumbo before they decided to earn their living in the great outdoors.

London's beggars are still emulating the wily Joseph Johnson today. You can see them with their dogs in doorways, outside and inside Underground railway stations, and most of the animals look pitiful. Each time I notice one I think of Circe and the melancholy expression she assumed when she was temporarily deprived of a sock or ball. Perhaps we could have amassed a tidy fortune together, similar to that enjoyed by Billy Walters or by Joseph Johnson and his succession of faithful Tobys.

Una Vita Nuova

'Circe understands Italian,' Vanni remarked with a grin. He had been caring for her while I had taken a week's holiday in Egypt. 'She's a dumb linguist, thanks to me.'

It was true, after a fashion. In seven days she had learnt that *Vieni qui*, spoken with authority, was the same as 'Come here', and that *Giù* meant 'Get down'. She understood, too, that when Vanni said *Cattiva* it was to indicate that she was behaving badly, and *Tu sei bella*, accompanied by a gentle pat, could only mean that she was beautiful and on her best behaviour. She was now, perhaps, the only bilingual dog in the park.

Vanni attended David's funeral and stayed with me for some weeks afterwards. We had been friends, the three of us, since the spring of 1968. Earlier that year, I had been given an award for my first novel, and one of the conditions of the prize was – and still is – that the money be spent abroad. (I had planned to go to Rome, and was taking Italian lessons from an elderly man who lived in a gloomy basement flat near Baker Street. He only once spoke to me in English during the six-week course. 'Hullo,' he said as he opened the door when I arrived for my first lesson. 'This is the last English you will hear. *Buon giorno.*') But Vanni persuaded me to stay in Florence, his native city. I would meet his family and friends, and improve my Italian.

I flew to Pisa, and waited an eternity for my luggage. It was not forthcoming. An airline official told me, with a calmness I found exasperating, that the flight had gone on to Singapore, with my suitcase in the hold. I could collect it, he assured me, in three days, when the next Singapore–Pisa–London trip was scheduled. Accompanied by Vanni and another new friend, Paolo, I travelled by train to Florence, where Paolo had found me a wonderful room at the very top of the Hotel Paris on Via dei Banchi, a minute's walk from the railway station. I stayed there for three happy months, paying a pittance for my eyrie.

I needed a change of shirt, some socks and underwear. To my amazement, the underpants cost almost as much as the shirt and socks combined. I had told the shop assistant that I required *mutande*, but did not realize until I opened the box that the *mutande* he had sold me were made of *seta*. I had bought four pairs of silk slips, all of which disintegrated in the hotel's washing machine.

Paolo happened to be with me when the man from Alitalia phoned to say that my luggage was in Pisa, awaiting collection. Paolo seized the phone and reminded the man that it was because of his company's inefficiency that my case had ended up in Singapore. The case was delivered to the hotel later that afternoon.

It was thanks to Vanni, who was to become an expert in Medieval French and Italian literature, and Paolo, an art historian, that I saw so many marvellous paintings, frescoes and sculptures during that first stay. They were the most informative, the most lucid, of guides. It was Vanni who introduced me to that remarkable hillside church, San Miniato al Monte, with its quasi-oriental decorations on the inlaid pavement in the nave and on the walls of the monks' choir. The mosaics of various beasts and of the signs of the zodiac reached Florence from Byzantium at the time of the Crusades.

One unforgettable September morning Paolo took me to see the frescoes in the Brancacci Chapel in the church of Santa Maria del Carmine. So dark was it in the chapel that coins had to be fed constantly into a machine to ensure a few moments of light in which to gawp at the marvels before us. The paintings by Masolini and Lippi are graceful and exquisitely composed, but those by Masaccio are on an altogether more exalted plane. The apostles in *Tribute Money* have a sculptured gravity and seem to be in possession of a rich inner life. Masolino's *Temptation* of Adam and Eve is beautiful enough, but the couple in Masaccio's *Expulsion from the Garden* on the opposite wall are human beings racked with unendurable pain and grief. They are raw in their misery. In 1968, Adam's genitals were hidden behind a fig leaf some prude had painted on in the eighteenth century. After the detailed and precise work of restoration of the frescoes that was financed by the Olivetti corporation throughout the 1980s, Adam's cock and balls are visible at last. The *Expulsion* is one of the greatest artistic manifestations of the perils in store for suffering humanity. Masaccio (Tommaso di Ser Giovanni) was a working-class boy. *Accio* is a suffix meaning rude, rough or dirty. Perhaps this colossal genius, who died at the age of twenty-six, merited the sobriquet 'rough trade'.

Vanni and Paolo came from very different backgrounds. Vanni, whose nose resembled that of Federigo da Montefeltro, Count of Urbino, in the portrait by Piero della Francesca in the Uffizi, came from artisan stock, whilst Paolo could boast that he was born into one of Siena's oldest aristocratic families. (There is a vault in the Duomo bearing the family name.) Everyone remarked that Paolo's way of speaking was *raffinato*. It certainly sounded posher, to my untrained ears, than the other voices I was listening to, with their Florentine habit of converting a hard 'c' into an 'h' of the Spanish kind. ('Coca-Cola' becomes, almost, 'hoha-hola'.) Paolo's vowels and consonants had none of these local impurities.

Some evenings we would meet for a drink in Florence's one openly gay bar, which was cast in the form of an English pub called the George and Dragon. A blond American, much sought after by the more obvious queens, pretended not to notice the surrounding campery as he served beer and spirits. He may have been an innocent, that farmer's son from Wisconsin, working his way through Europe. He looked at the swishing and mincing young Italians imperviously, neither smiling nor frowning at their antics. By this time, Vanni, Paolo and I were talking an idiotic cod Italian. We invented newly discovered operas – *Emilia di Wisconsin* by Donizetti and *La pudenda abbandonata* by Cimarosa – and ludicrous verbs such as *swishare* and *minciare*. As Vanni and I were leaving the unlikely pub one evening, Paolo entered with an American girl he was teaching Italian and the history of art. Inspired by a glass too many, I greeted him with the question '*Hai swishato stasera?*' ('Have you swished this evening?') The eager New Yorker, keen to learn the language as best she could, shrieked at Paolo, '*Swishato? Swishato?* What kind of word is that?' Paolo blushed – he was a natural blusher – and muttered something about *uno scherzo*, a joke. Vanni and I exited smiling.

Vanni had told his mother he was homosexual. She was distressed to begin with, but eventually came to terms with the fact, especially when he became involved in a relationship. Poor Paolo could not afford, literally, to be as honest. He lived in fear that his parents would discover the truth about him. He was the youngest son in a large family – I seem to recall that he had innumerable siblings, most of them sisters. His father, who was then in his late seventies, was threatening to deprive Paolo of his inheritance if he didn't marry. The old man repeated the threat whenever he was ill, which was often. I still don't know if it was the thought of losing a considerable legacy that caused Paolo to become engaged to the attractive and highly intelligent Parisienne he later married. I met the newlyweds in London, and the cagey Paolo gave the impression – a very understandable impression, given his wife's beauty and intellect – that he was much in love.

I was living in Fargo, North Dakota, in the late 1970s when Vanni rang me from Oakland in California with the terrible news that Paolo had died of a heart attack at the age of thirty-two. This was bad enough, but not quite as awful as the reality, which I would learn about in Florence in 1980. The heart-attack story had been concocted by Paolo's widow to ease the pain his parents were suffering. It transpired that she had undergone an abortion, and that Paolo – ever the devout, if once wayward, Catholic – had been upset and horrified. Was this the reason for his suicide? It is hard, and perhaps impertinent, to speculate. The truth is that on a summer afternoon, when his wife was out working – she was a skilled translator and interpreter – Paolo leapt from the balcony of their fifth-floor apartment in Paris. It was an ugly and brutal death for my sweet friend, *l'uomo raffinato*.

His body was transported to Siena. A traditional Catholic funeral was held in a parish church. After the burial, Paolo's widow returned to France and disappeared from the lives of her husband's friends and relatives. I assume she wanted no more reminders of him. That seems the likeliest explanation.

*

In the late 1960s, Vanni's family was in thrall to his paternal grandmother. La Nonna had been widowed early in her marriage and had raised her only son, Piero, single-handedly. She was a formidable presence, especially in the kitchen, from which everyone was banned when she was cooking in earnest. Once, trying to thank her for the delicious *polpettone* she had served us, I got my words mixed up and praised her *ciondolone* (meaning idler or drifter) instead. Her normally stern features cracked into a smile, and then she joined in the laughter round the table.

She loved, and was loved by, the entire family, even when her temper was at its most severe. She had but one enemy as far as I could see, and she certainly made her loathing of him evident. The object of her antipathy was Il Nonno, Vanni's maternal grandfather, who also lived in the large apartment. La Nonna and Il Nonno rarely communicated, and then only in grunts. She had to cook separate dishes for him, because the old man had problems with his digestion. He supped on various kinds of *brodo*, bowls of which she set before him with scarcely disguised contempt.

Why did she hate him so? Perhaps it was because his life had not been as hard as hers. Yet both survived the Nazi occupation, as had her son and Il Nonno's daughter, Noris. Filial duty ensured that the domineering Nonna and the quiet, ineffectual Nonno – who was occupied for hours each day with those books of puzzles the Italians enjoy so much – should have to put up with one another's company.

I happened to be in Florence, staying in the apartment, when La Nonna was dying. I was ushered briefly into her presence. The forceful woman of two years earlier was frail now and worn out, but she smiled on recognizing me and called me 'Paulo'.

In the summer of 1986, Vanni and I often talked of those early years of our friendship as we exercised Circe in the park. I reminded him of that time, shortly after my arrival in Florence, when my feet were blistered from walking on cobbled streets. I asked him if there was an Italian equivalent of the liquid antiseptic TCP (which my mother 'swore by', as they say) and, looking puzzled, he replied 'TBC'. I was unaware that TBC is shorthand for tuberculosis. Thus it was that I entered a pharmacy and told the man behind the counter that I wanted a bottle of TBC.

'What for?' He grinned as he spoke.

'For my sore feet, naturally.'

He laughed, and then explained what TBC meant, and produced a cream which he said would heal my blisters.

This was the most lunatic of the lunatic conversations I had in Italy in the autumn of 1968.

We talked of La Nonna and how, when it was raining – it rains a lot in Florence – she would smile at me and observe *Come Londra*. She had never visited London, but was convinced it was a city above which the skies were perpetually opening when it wasn't shrouded in fog. The wetness and fogginess of my birthplace were incontrovertible facts, carved out in the stone of centuries. It was useless to argue with her.

Vanni was teaching in the Italian department in the prestigious University of California at Berkeley while I was helping the freshmen (and women) at North Dakota State University unravel the mysteries of English grammar. I visited him twice in California. I had gone there to interview the novelist Christopher Isherwood for BBC Radio, and Christopher had picked me up at Los Angeles airport and driven me in his tiny Volkswagen to Santa Monica, where he lived with his partner, the artist Don Bachardy. We recorded our discussion about his life and work in a nearby studio that afternoon. The engineer in charge was a huge man who greeted us warmly as 'Chris' and 'Paul'. He was friendly before the conversation started, but Christopher's answer to my first question caused him to be distinctly unfriendly when we were due to leave.

Me: Christopher Isherwood, why did you go to Berlin in the early 1930s?

CI: For the boys.

I persevered with my next question, even as I sensed a certain frostiness from the other side of the glass partition. The redneck didn't like what he was hearing. Christopher went on chirping happily about his career, and I tried not to look at the man who was recording the programme. We were not addressed as 'Chris' and 'Paul' as we walked out to the car park. An hour earlier we had been 'regular guys', but not any more. We were a pair of English faggots now. His expression said as much.

In those days, San Francisco was the gay capital of America, if not the world. I found the city exhilarating and beautiful, especially after the fearful cold of Fargo and the endless flatness of the snow-covered plains. Although it was December, the weather was mild and walking in the sunlit streets and riding on the cable cars were rare but simple pleasures. Vanni showed me the sights, and the two of us spent an afternoon in the Castro district, which was predominantly gay. I found the atmosphere of the place as curious as it was depressing. I had never seen quite so many men with cropped hair and neat moustaches, who appeared to have nothing to do but cruise the bars in search of their lookalikes. This was a new, and strange, kind of narcissism. We were in a self-styled ghetto, I realized, and I couldn't wait to get out of it. I was happy in the multi-cultured city itself, with its limitless choice of fine restaurants. In Tommaso's we ate the best pizza to be had outside Naples.

I went to Berkeley with Vanni and met the Italian faculty. At a party there, a bearded man wearing a kaftan and an assortment of beads informed me confidently that he was going to write the greatest of all great American novels. Had he started it? 'Not yet.' He put a finger to his forehead. 'It's still up here.' I remarked, as tactfully as I could, that he didn't look *that* young, and that when you have embarked on a novel, great or otherwise, time was important. Life is an accidental business, and illness and death are out there, ready to do their worst. He gave me a pitying smile. 'Are you some kind of a pessimist? I just *know* when my book is going to come out. It's still . . .' He searched for the apt word. '. . . *marinating*.'

A real writer had graced the campus earlier that year, in the form of Giorgio Bassani, author of *The Garden of the Finzi-Continis*. I love Bassani's fictions, autobiographical in essence, of Jewish – and other – life in Ferrara in the years preceding the Second World War. Vanni admired them too, but the man turned out to be snobbish and charmless to an extraordinary degree. He refused to drink Californian wine, and had his own vintages sent over from Italy. He was in his fifties, but continued to play accomplished tennis. He sulked whenever he was in danger of losing a match. He was rude to both staff and students, some of whom he deemed stupid. He had been hired for two years as writer-in-residence. When he had completed his first year, he was paid another year's salary to go home. It had been a bitter experience for everyone. Yet his elegant, mournful books endure, and we have him to thank for discovering and publishing Lampedusa's *Il Gattopardo* (literally The Cheetah, but famously translated as *The Leopard*). And no one deserves the fate of his last decades, when he was afflicted with Parkinson's disease and Alzheimer's.

On a second trip to California, during the spring vacation, Vanni and I hired a car from a firm called Rent-a-Dent in Los Angeles and we set off to visit the original Forest Lawn Memorial Park, the setting of Evelyn Waugh's novel *The Loved One*. Our journey along the freeway was hindered by the driver of a large truck who kept overtaking our battered saloon with a glee that bordered on the murderous. We wondered if we would ever reach the famous cemetery alive, so determined seemed the truck driver to force us off the road. There had been three crashes that morning, we learned, and we didn't want to be involved in the fourth. It was with huge relief that we spotted the exit for Glendale.

The cemetery more than lived up to (if that's the appropriate term) our anticipation of the comic possibilities ahead. The first thing we discovered was that words like 'undertaker' and 'mortician' had been replaced with 'before need counselor'. The founder of Forest Lawn, Dr Hubert Eaton, had paid for the acres of barren land in 1917 by selling plots on a hire purchase system. Hence those 'before need counselors'. We parked the car, and began our tour by visiting the Little Church of the Flowers, modelled on the church in Stoke Poges that inspired Thomas Gray to write his 'Elegy'. From there, we went on to the Wee Kirk o' the Heather (that o' was cause for a smile), a replica of the kirk in Glencairn where Annie Laurie worshipped. We entered, and left, to the accompaniment of bagpipes. We gave the Church of the Recessional (a reproduction of St Margaret's in Rottingdean, which Rudyard Kipling attended) a miss and made our way to God's Garden, in which is enshrined another replica – that of a statue of Christ by the Danish sculptor Bertel Thorvaldsen. We were in the Court of the Christus within God's Garden, staring at the bearded Christ, when a recorded voice came out of a tree. 'You are standing before the Son of God' it boomed. 'If you wish to look into his eyes, you must go down on your knees.' We did as instructed, and duly caught His bland expression.

'You are standing in the Westminster Abbey of the New World' another booming voice announced as we stepped into the Memorial Court of Honor. That same sepulchral voice instructed us – there was one other person present, a woman with a nervous tic – to take our seats if we wished to see, and learn the history of, the *Last Supper* Window. The lights dimmed and a pair of curtains parted to the strains of the waltz from *The Merry Widow*. On the screen was Leonardo da Vinci's *Last Supper* in its frail state of preservation. Then the voice explained that Dr Hubert Eaton had visited Milan in the 1920s and had been awestruck by the sight of the painting. It grieved Dr Hubert Eaton that Leonardo's masterwork was so faint, due to the ravages of time. The doctor had an inspiration. He contacted 'famed artist' Rosa Moretti and asked what she would give to make a stained-glass replica of the *Last Supper*. 'I would give my life, Dr Eaton,' she replied.

We began to laugh, Vanni and I, as the voice droned on, imparting the news that Rosa Moretti produced her stained-glass window only to have it crack. And where did it crack? With the figure of Judas. She telephoned Dr Hubert Eaton, who encouraged her to try again. She finished a second window and a crack appeared in exactly the same place. A third window cracked, and so did the fourth and fifth. It was as though Judas, the betrayer of Our Lord, had put a curse on it. Rosa Moretti was very unhappy. Dr Hubert Eaton telephoned 'famed artist' (hearing that phrase once more, we collapsed with laughter) Rosa Moretti and advised her to pray. He would pray, too, for the window he had commissioned. Their joint prayers might save the day. So Dr Hubert Eaton in California and Rosa Moretti in Perugia offered up their prayers for a perfect window. Their prayers were answered, and Dr Hubert Eaton and Rosa Moretti were overjoyed. They had won their battle with the wicked spirit of Judas Iscariot.

The brightly coloured *Last Supper* Window was revealed to us, to the accompaniment of the *Blue Danube*.

'Do you guys come here just to break up?' the woman asked, as we were overcome with giggling. 'Have either of you been to Italy?' she enquired, pointing to a copy of Michelangelo's *Pietà* in St Peter's.

I said that my friend was Italian.

'Have you seen the original *Pietà* (she pronounced it pee-*ay*-ter) in Rome?'

We both answered that we had.

'Doesn't the Virgin Mary have a sort of strip across her body?'

'Yes, she does,' we replied.

'It's not here,' she shrieked. 'Look.' We looked. The strip wasn't there. 'It's a fake. This is not a real replica. I shall write to the *Los Angeles Times*. I shall write to the Pope.' And thus shrieking, she stormed out of the Westminster Abbey of the New World.

We were on the verge of hysteria. The *Blue Danube* faded away. There was a moment's silence before *The Ride of the Valkyries* began. *The Ride of the Valkyries?* Was there a humourist lurking in the recesses of the Memorial Court of Honor?

Later that day, we inspected the replica of Ghiberti's bronze doors from the Baptistery of San Giovanni, saw Michelangelo's newly fig-leafed David, and took in Jan Styka's huge painting *The Crucifixion* (complete with recorded comments from the hecklers in the crowd) and *The Resurrection* by Robert Clark, which is almost as huge and just as dire. We chanced on a sculpture depicting several generations of men, women and children entitled *The Mystery of Life* and were hysterical once more when the song

> Ah, sweet mystery of life
> At last I've found you,
> Ah, sweet mystery of life
> At last you're mine

started to be sung by an unseen choir nearby.

We got back into the car and drove slowly through Lullaby Land, the section of Forest Lawn in which the very young are buried. Recorded birdsong was coming out of every bush, and childish voices were singing or reciting nursery rhymes. We were beyond laughter now. We had to escape the sound of those innocents telling us of Jack and Jill, and Humpty Dumpty, and the Old Woman Who Lived in a Shoe.

★

Vanni had some news that he didn't want to break over the phone. Could he spend a few days with me? That, I said, was an unnecessary question.

Circe, tail wagging in delight, rushed to greet her friend as soon as he arrived. *Carissima* he called her, and allowed her to lick his face. We went into the kitchen and I opened a bottle of white wine. He needed a drink before he could tell me what he had come to say face to face. The dog wrapped herself about his feet.

'It's the worst. It's what I've been afraid of for years.'

I was silent, waiting for the revelation I had somehow already anticipated.

'I am HIV positive.'

We shared a long embrace.

Vanni would entrust himself to the care of Dario, the youngest of his two younger brothers. Dario would soon become what he is now, the leading AIDS specialist in Florence. Since Dario had access to every new drug the moment it was patented, it was possible for him to give Vanni the best treatment available. Vanni was already taking pills when he turned up that day with his upsetting news. He stayed well, and sane, and active in his job as a tour guide for over five years.

He came to London in 1996, but did not stay with me and my partner, Jeremy. To my surprise, he had booked himself into an expensive hotel in Curzon Street. The idea of Vanni living it up in Mayfair struck me as preposterous, and indeed it was. On what would turn out to be his last holiday, Vanni indulged himself in a bizarre shopping spree. He bought eighty-two pairs of Armani underpants (*Perché ottanta-due?* became something of a family joke), ten cashmere sweaters, a dozen identical overcoats and six suitcases to contain them. He was washing down his medication with an excess of red wine. Jeremy and I spent an evening with him, bearing him back to the hotel after a meal in a Chinese restaurant. He insisted on a goodnight drink, but we – and the courteous hotel staff – insisted otherwise.

I had to leave for Germany the next day. Jeremy dined with him again. Vanni was copiously and uncontrollably sick at the table, but the staff in the restaurant were considerate, kind and diplomatic, swiftly clearing up the mess while Jeremy helped him to wash and clean himself in the lavatory.

Some while before this, Jeremy and I had spent Christmas with the family in Florence, and – accompanied by Jeremy's mother – travelled from Rome to have lunch with them the following December. On both occasions, Vanni had appeared alert and relatively happy, joining in the conversation, swapping anecdotes, and commenting intelligently on the always-parlous state of Italian politics. But the desperate Vanni we saw in London was a different man. He was confident to the point of boastfulness, and we assumed that the combination of drink and drugs accounted for his erratic behaviour. We could not know that his decline into dementia had just begun.

Vanni had been given a credit card by his father, and in Amsterdam, the next stop on his travels, he went over the agreed limit – which was pretty generous, anyway. His brother Geri drove to Holland and took the untypical spendthrift home. He was not to be released again.

In the autumn of 1998, Jeremy and I had a weekend holiday in Florence, staying in a beautiful hotel (a former villa of Mussolini's) in the hills above Piazzale Michelangelo. We called in on the family. Wine had been banished from the apartment, because even the scent of it caused Vanni irritated temptation. He was confined to his room, where we sat with him. His whole body was wasted, and his naturally large eyes loomed ever larger in his sunken face. He was watching an idiotic game show on the television, laughing at the crass jokes. He had lost all memory of his crazy last outing. It was impossible to talk of serious matters with him. Here was a man who had once recited whole passages of Dante and entire sonnets by Petrarch from memory reduced to a merrily gibbering wreck. At one point, the game show was interrupted by a news bulletin, giving details of a train crash. Vanni averted his eyes from the screen. Death was not to be contemplated.

Vanni phoned me at intervals, saying that he would be coming to London to stay with us. The first time he called, I wondered if Dario had effected a miracle. I rang Dario, who confirmed that no miracle had taken place. It was his brother's happy delusion that he could travel. His last call was in 2001, some weeks before his death.

I was in Padua in June 2001, intent on visiting the family in Vada, the seaside town where they have an apartment. I should have booked a train ticket in advance, because there was no possibility of a connection on the Sunday I had chosen for my visit. Every Eurostar train was full. So my last sight of my beloved friend of thirty years was in his room, with the game show in the background.

'*Ha lasciato,*' said Noris, his mother, when I phoned in December to ask how he was faring. 'He's left' – it's a touching euphemism for 'dead'.

In January 2002, I was in Rome for a week, meeting up with two Romanian friends. I went to Florence, and bought twelve gladioli – Noris's favourite flowers – before going to the familiar apartment. Noris took four of the gladioli and put them in a separate vase. They were for Vanni's room, she said. Would I take them in? Vanni's books were on the shelves, and on his desk was a framed photograph of him at the age of thirty or so, when he had the world before him.

I chatted with Noris as she prepared lunch. I was offered a glass of wine. There was a *grande vuoto* (a great emptiness) in their lives, Noris said. Noris and Piero had cared for their demanding first-born – with some necessary assistance from nurses – for five loving years.

I sat down to lunch with Noris, Piero, Dario and Dario's daughter, Martina. We reminisced and smiled at happy, and indeed silly (the dish of *ciondolone*) memories. Dario speaks with a thick Florentine accent, and Noris interrupted him once, requesting him to translate what he was saying into Italian for my benefit.

After lunch, I sat with Piero, while Noris – who had been a teacher of Italian, Latin and Greek in *liceo* – helped Martina with her studies in the dining room. Martina was required to learn a passage of Dante by heart, and Noris was now correcting her mistakes and prompting her when she faltered. Piero and I stopped talking, only to hear the sixteen-year-old reciting the heartbreaking words of the doomed Francesca from the fifth canto of *Inferno*:

> *Nessun maggior dolore*
> *che ricordarsi del tempo felice*
> *nela miseria . . .*

(There is no greater sorrow than to remember in misery the happy time . . .)

As we listened to her bright voice, I looked up to see Piero weeping softly. He was remembering, he said, Vanni the brilliant schoolboy learning those very lines at the same table where Martina was sitting.

Giovanna's Marshal Tito

Circe was not afraid of other dogs, even those who were obviously untrained or vicious. A snarling Staffordshire bull terrier was less terrifying than its belligerent owner, who threatened to knife me for releasing her into the Dogs Only area while his pet was exercising. I explained, temperately, that I hadn't seen either him or his dog when I had opened the gate. (I refrained from adding that I had not anticipated meeting two such ferocious beasts in my local park.) I withdrew Circe from the area, as the latterday Bill Sikes, whose beefy arms were lavishly tattooed, continued to abuse me in brutally basic language.

Only Giovanna's cat had the power to instil terror in the otherwise fearless Circe. This mountainous tabby, whose name was Marshal Tito, first startled her when she was a few months old by suddenly dashing out of Giovanna's front garden, arching his back, exposing his claws and hissing loudly. Circe let out a yelp and immediately backed away from the angry Tito, who seemed to be defying us to pass. From that day onwards, Circe always came to a determined halt some yards ahead of Tito's home. I had to lead her across the road – she led me, actually – to the pavement opposite, where the tom cat seldom lurked.

Tito's life was charmed, as his size testified. He was the most pampered animal in the neighbourhood, often to be seen spread out on the central windowsill, sleeping the sleep of the glutted. Giovanna fed her beloved tabby whenever he indicated that a meal would be welcome, his raucous miaowing silenced with offerings of freshly cooked fish or chicken. Marshal Tito was a gourmand, thanks to her tender solicitations.

I came to know Giovanna in a curious manner. A friend, who lived two doors along from her, told her of my interest in Italy, which I visited as often as I could, and that I spoke Italian. I was putting the rubbish out one morning just as Giovanna was turning the corner, walking stick in hand. '*Buon giorno,*' she called out to me, and I replied in kind. Then she stopped at the gate and said something truly alarming to me, a stranger. '*Mio marito non mi chiave adesso,*' she confided. Had I heard correctly? I stared at her in astonishment. '*Davvero?*' I asked. '*Si, davvero,*' she responded. '*Certo.*' She was telling me what I didn't wish to hear – that her husband no longer fucked her. She had chosen the verb *chiavare* rather than the more sedate *fare amore*, which would have suggested a falling out of love instead of a refusal to satisfy her physical needs. I was embarrassed by this revelation, though I did not say so. In the years of our friendship, she never repeated it. We talked of different, infinitely sadder, things.

Giovanna ruled, or tried to rule, over a troubled household. Her sexually inadequate husband's face was set in a permanent scowl. He spent his days in the streets, out of the sight and sound of the wife he loathed. He spoke solely to himself at all times, in a mixture of Ukrainian and English. When he came home at night, he slumped in his chair, Giovanna informed me, and slept. He wasted none of his precious words on his sons, Andrea and Enrico, except to shout at them occasionally, when they presumed to address him.

Ivan was born and raised in Kiev. He arrived in England as a young man in the late 1930s. He worked for a considerable period as a sous chef in one of the grand London hotels, but was sacked after his excessive drinking became problematic. He met Giovanna, who came from a small town in the Veneto, and whose first job in England was as a maid at Eton College. Their house in the west London street where I still live has four storeys, so they must have been doing reasonably well when they moved in during the 1950s. It is hard for me to imagine the desiccated Ivan and the grossly fat Giovanna, her legs swollen from rheumatism, as ever being youthful and attractive, so cruelly had circumstances treated them.

Why did they never separate? Giovanna was staunchly Catholic, and the idea of divorce was not countenanced. In a peculiar sense, they were separate in each other's unacknowledged company, as they sat night after night – she staring at the television; he snoozing, or remaining stubbornly silent, in his chair – like two characters out of Strindberg performing in dumbshow. I learned of this bizarre domestic routine from Giovanna, as she stooped to stroke Circe, whom she called *la bella cagna*. I learned, too, of her younger son's drug addiction and his battles with the police, and that her eldest boy, who had once been happily married, was now back with his doting mother. He was the only member of the family, apart from Tito, who really appreciated her cooking. His English wife had murdered the pasta he loved.

Giovanna introduced me to Andrea, her *bello ragazzo*, who instantly turned 'Paul' into 'Paolo'. I was Paolo thereafter. He was invariably cheerful as he jabbered in Italian or English of banal concerns, yet I quickly detected that behind his sunniness was someone seriously disturbed. He had a slight hold on reality, I discovered – the cause, perhaps, of the failure of his brief marriage. He reminded me, and continues to do so, of those unworldly, childlike grown-ups in Dickens's novels – Mr Dick in *David Copperfield*; Fanny Cleaver, alias 'Jenny Wren' in *Our Mutual Friend*; even the pathetic Smike in *Nicholas Nickleby*. He had lost certain essential bearings, and needed Giovanna's protection, as much as she – it transpired – needed his. He was a beaming outcast in that world in which most of us function. He probably still is.

There was nothing sunny about Enrico, who was known as Rico to the addicts and drunks who were his frequent companions. He was surly and short-tempered, given to sudden rages when he was not brooding on whatever was obsessing him – his next heroin fix, more likely than not. He would disappear for months at a stretch and then return to torment his mother, now almost wholly reliant on the support of Andrea. The police, to Giovanna's understandable distress, were regular visitors to the house, especially when Rico was missing. Giovanna was not at all happy when her renegade son brought Alison, an ex-prostitute, home with him. He took her to his bedroom, which she occupied when she wasn't in detention or prison. Alison's command of language was severely limited, like that of the owner of the Staffordshire bull terrier, to one or two oft-repeated expletives.

Silent and sullen misery was now replaced by high drama. Alison and Rico screamed at each other with such ferocity that Ivan felt compelled to join in. Once, during yet another of Rico's mysterious absences, Giovanna bolted the front door against Alison, who eventually availed herself of a brick which she hurled through a window. The police carted her off, to the echoing cries of her favourite word, which were aimed at the sick and increasingly desperate woman who lived in dread of becoming her mother-in-law.

With Rico on his travels and Alison locked up, peace of a kind descended on the house again. Giovanna prepared delicious meals for Andrea and Marshal Tito, and the single annoyance to cope with, by way of ignoring him, was her moody husband, who returned every night to sulk or sleep. The former chef ate in a workmen's café in Shepherd's Bush when he felt like eating, but he was generally sustained by the gin he consumed in amazing quantities, to judge by the empty bottles he deposited in the litter bins in Ravenscourt Park, where I exercised Circe each morning and afternoon.

I was in the park on one particular afternoon, chatting to quite the most elegant of the Bone People (as we dog lovers described ourselves) when our conversation was interrupted by something stirring in a nearby bush. Thelma, the wife of a QC and the daughter of an officer in the Indian army, went over to investigate. It was then that Ivan emerged, with his ancient raincoat (so ancient that the original brown material had turned green in places) completely unbuttoned. Thelma, casting a cold eye on that part of his body Ivan had denied Giovanna for decades, remarked calmly, 'Oh, do put that beastly thing away. It's not a pretty sight', and walked back to me with the question – 'What were we discussing? A rather wholesome subject, wasn't it?'

Rico came home, and was joined by Alison. 'My son with a *puttana*', Giovanna spat out in the course of our last meeting. Between them, Rico and his blonde, loud-mouthed lover now contrived to upset the old woman in as nasty a fashion as can be conceived. The friend, Kitty, who had told Giovanna of my interest in Italian culture, offered to help Rico who was, as usual, unemployed. Kitty invited him to paint the walls of her sitting room, and a generous fee was agreed on. Rico, aided by Alison, took on the job. While Kitty and her husband, Rupert, were out, Rico stole some money from Kitty's purse and Alison picked up a silver bowl, which she carried round to the antique-cum-junk shop run by Dennis, a smiling Jamaican with a glistening gold tooth. Dennis gave her £30 for it, realizing it was worth more. He sold it to a stranger for £300 that same afternoon. The bowl had been given to Kitty by an aunt who had had the forethought to insure it. As a consequence, Kitty collected thousands of pounds and bought a new car. But Giovanna was mortified.

Worse was to ensue. Rico, Alison and a trio of drunks were having a Special Brew party in an upstairs room. It was decided that they would play poker. One of the men said he would prefer to watch, and duly sat on a sofa, clutching his can. The poker players were not suspicious of his sustained silence and later assumed he had fallen asleep. As morning approached, Rico started to shake him and then realized he was dead, though he maintained a firm grip on the can. The corpse was removed, and Giovanna asked her God what He was thinking of to bring such pain and suffering and shame into her life.

She died soon after, and so did Ivan, and then Marshal Tito shook off his substantial mortal coil. Andrea, who had appeared to be stoical about his parents' deaths, was deeply hurt by Tito's passing. He told all the shopkeepers in the district and many of the neighbours, including me, that his lovely cat had gone.

How do you let a dog know that her arch-enemy no longer exists? You can't. I couldn't. The ghost of Marshal Tito plagued Circe for the rest of her life. We went on crossing the road, to keep clear of the fat dictator. For eleven years, Marshal Tito was a malign immortal as far as my beautiful bitch – *la bella cagna* – was concerned.

Mumm's the Word

Jeremy and I were watching a television documentary about Radovan Karadžić – the self-styled poet, self-proclaimed 'leader' of the Bosnian Serbs, and erstwhile psychologist to the Sarajevo football team – when a familiar figure came on the screen. Who was this clown in army fatigues pretending to be a soldier? 'I know that man,' I said. And then, as he began to drool over Karadžić, telling his hero he was another Alexander the Great, but greater, I saw the dreaded name: Edward Limonov. It made sense to me that Limonov should be worshipping at the feet of a mass murderer.

In May 1989, I took part in a conference in Budapest attended by some of the world's finest writers. The event was sponsored by the Getty Foundation in America. We were put up in the Budapest Hilton and treated with lavish hospitality.

During that week, the body of Imre Nagy, one of the martyrs of the 1956 uprising, was reburied in his rightful grave. Hundreds of people were at the cemetery to witness this belated act of mercy. For all the evident grief and sadness on display, there was also a patent feeling of hope and renewal in the air. The sun was shining, and the city streets were thronged with young men and women who appeared to be happier and healthier and better dressed than their counterparts in Romania. It was almost as if the Wall had already crumbled.

The conference began, as conferences do, with welcoming speeches from our hosts at a ceremonial dinner. Then, for the next five days, there were sessions every morning and afternoon. The Germans concentrated on the likely possibility of a united Germany and what it implied in literary terms; the French were philosophical, and Alain Robbe-Grillet, a mischievous wit and raconteur away from the podium, droned on at length on that unappealing subject, The Death of the Novel; the Indians were sweet-natured, and talked of many poets and storytellers – most of them Bengali – whose works had never been translated; the speakers from Eastern Europe, who included the remarkable Danilo Kiš, who was shortly to die of cancer, were sceptical rather than optimistic about the future; the Africans looked forward to the end of apartheid in South Africa, and Nadine Gordimer mentioned several promising black writers unknown in Europe and the United States, and the Americans seemed to agree that the days of the ubiquitous Great American Novel were over. The British contingent were ill at ease, because the author appointed to make the address, David Pryce-Jones, took the opportunity to trash contemporary English fiction for not being seriously involved with political issues. But our disapproval of Pryce-Jones was as nothing to that exhibited by the Arabs and Israelis for each other's points of view. Here was real drama – stormy exits from the conference hall, angry accusations from the floor, and desperate pleas for common sense and respect for literature to prevail.

Edward Limonov was a late arrival, taking his fellow Russians – who loathed him – by surprise. He had been living in Paris, where he had written the punk autobiographical novel *It's Me, Eddie*. His reason for being in Budapest, it seemed, was to insult the Hungarians by praising the Russian soldiers who were sent in to thwart the possible revolution in

1956. He was unstoppable in his condemnation of all the countries in the Soviet bloc. He was not consistent, though. If he was attacking those nations for anti-Semitism and other forms of racism, why did he turn his venom on the Jews? And, indeed, the Arabs? He was playing the role of anarchist, antagonist and denigrator of the status quo up to, and beyond, the very hilt. He was twice evicted from meetings, when he was dragged out screaming.

On the last day of the conference a representative from each country was chosen to thank the hosts and to offer a few general comments. I was elected to speak on behalf of the British writers, and I said how moved we had been by the scenes at the cemetery and how much we had enjoyed the experience of seeing Budapest and meeting poets, novelists and historians we had hitherto admired from afar. There had been only one severely disruptive influence, but I would desist from naming him.

Limonov knew who I was referring to, as did everyone present. That night we had a party on a boat cruising up and down the Danube. I danced with Madame Robbe-Grillet, who was encased, as ever, in tight-fitting black leather. It was long after midnight when we returned to the hotel, where a small group of us – Angela Carter, Richard Ford, Amitav Ghosh, Gianni Celati, Christopher Hope and myself – decided to order champagne as a farewell nightcap. The Russians, minus Limonov, were seated nearby, drinking beer and vodka.

We were into the second bottle of Mumm when Limonov appeared, wild-eyed and spoiling for a fight with anyone. He clearly intended that I was to be that anyone. He strode over to my chair and looked down at me.

'Are you for or against capital punishment?'

'That's a strange question to ask at two in the morning,' I replied.

'Answer me,' he demanded. 'For or against?'

'I'm against it, of course.'

'I thought so, you fucking Western liberal.'

I took a breath, and said, 'What is it with you? You've been foul to everybody all week. Do you have a problem? Are you by any chance a closet transvestite?'

Hearing this, Limonov picked up the empty champagne bottle and struck me on the head.

I can't recall how long I was unconscious. There were scuffles. The Russians darted over to our table, grabbed Limonov and threw him into the lift. When I had come to, the biggest of the Russians asked me what I had done to annoy Limonov. I told him, and he thanked and embraced me.

'You were lucky it was a champagne bottle,' Angela remarked. 'A wine bottle might have broken.'

Limonov reappeared, shouting, 'Have I killed him? Have I killed him?' The Russians dispatched him again.

I had a sore head for weeks afterwards, and often had to lie down to ease the pain, with the ever-attentive Circe at my bedside.

So there was Limonov in the company of his hero, who invited him to use the machine-gun that had been strategically positioned to kill or injure as many innocents as possible in the city below. Limonov accepted the invitation fulsomely, spraying bullets indiscriminately, joyful at the prospect of polishing off a Muslim or two.

A decade after the incident in the Hilton, I visited Sarajevo. I met men and women and children with missing limbs, and several with a missing eye – the lasting mementoes of the gunfire that came at them from the surrounding hills, where Karadžić was now in hiding, protected by his private army. They all said how lucky they were to be alive.

In Banja Luka, two days later, I was shown Karadžić's office in the council building. His name was still on the door. Someone was expecting him back.

In the spring of 2002, Edward Limonov was in prison in Moscow, awaiting trial for drug-dealing and fraud.

Crime Passionnel

I somehow knew the woman was from Central or Eastern Europe before I discovered she was Polish. I attained that knowledge simply by observing the way she dressed. Her elegant clothes had a dated look about them – tailored suits in the lightest of tweeds; dainty, wasp-waisted jackets with fur collars; sequinned pink or mauve jumpers; crisply pleated skirts; shiny court shoes. I had seen such outfits on well-to-do women in Budapest, Prague, Bucharest and Warsaw. They conjured up a vanished conservative age, when fashion was muted rather than ostentatious. Her slightly podgy prettiness suggested a diet of sausage, dumplings, sauerkraut, roast pork and beer.

She came into the park with her dog, an Alsatian whose coat she brushed lovingly. She smiled and said good morning to everyone, but little more than that. She always looked as if she had just visited her hairdresser, for her dark brown hair was never less than perfectly coiffured. In winter, we regulars trudged through the mud in our wellington boots, but she wore galoshes over her shoes. She was shy and modest in her demeanour, yet she made an impression on us as she moved gracefully in our midst.

Adjacent to the roundabout near Ravenscourt Park is a stretch of grass known as Starch Green. It's a favoured haunt of the local alcoholics, who gather there all the year round. The star among them is Peggy, a volatile pensioner with an impressive collection of funny hats – a jester's cap with bells; a medieval liripipe; a gentleman's topper – who sings and dances lewdly before passing out. In June 1993, the Polish woman and the husband she had barred from their flat because of his own problems with drink walked towards Starch Green with their lustrous pet. The man had wanted to visit her, but she had insisted they discuss their differences in the open air. It was a balmy evening.

They sat on a bench on the green and talked. She was seen to rise, and then he produced a gun and shot her dead. He turned the gun on himself, collapsing beside her.

The police and paramedics were unable to remove the bodies. The dog wouldn't countenance them doing so. He was protecting both master and mistress, baring his teeth at anyone who came remotely near them. An hour passed. A dog-handler appeared, gently coaxing the distraught Alsatian to come to heel.

What was the dog expressing? The deepest devotion, I care to believe.

A Time in the Hills

There is a soup in Britain called Brown Windsor which tastes of nothing in particular. I think I last consumed it in Darjeeling in March 1994, but I can't be certain. It was set before me in the dining room of the Windamere Hotel, which the poet Dom Moraes had recommended to me, with a chuckle, as the only place in India that still served steak-and-kidney pudding. It looked brownish, and there were no suspect pieces of meat floating in it. Yet when I swallowed a spoonful I realized that it tasted of warm water, with the faintest suggestion of beef extract. The very faintest suggestion of beef extract.

Earlier that day, I had flown from Calcutta to Bagdogra, in the company of Mitalee Chatterjee from the British Council, an independent spirit who prefers jeans to the perpetual sari. She was wearing jeans for the flight and received many disbelieving stares from policemen, soldiers and airline staff. At Bagdogra it was necessary to have my passport stamped, since Darjeeling is, officially, in the kingdom of Nepal. I queued up outside a dusty, cobwebby hut, in which a pile of moth-eaten ledgers was perched on top of a dirty filing cabinet. An amiable Englishwoman, dressed in a sari neatly folded through Salvation Army epaulettes, remarked that the ledgers had been there, unopened, since 1947. It was like a scene from one of R. K. Narayan's novels or stories, for the three men on duty – two of whom entered our names and passport numbers in ledgers at the pace of a comatose snail, while the third pretended to be supervising – were blissfully oblivious of the anger and annoyance they were causing us. They took their time, and it seemed to last for ever.

Mitalee and I were driven up to Darjeeling in a Land Rover, the driver negotiating the narrow mountain roads with great skill. The air was crisp and cool, and a welcome change after the ferocious heat of Calcutta.

The Windamere is a former hill station. It consists of a main house, furnished and decorated in the style of the 1930s, and a series of chalets. From the moment I walked in to my chalet, I knew I was going to enjoy my stay. The notice in the frugal bathroom was enough to lift my spirits. I read:

NOTE

The chain-action water-closet in
this room has been giving dependable
service since 1912.

There were other notes to digest. I copied them into the diary I was keeping.

COFFEE BY WINDAMERE

From the Baba Budan Hills of Mysore in Southern India comes some of the finest coffee in the world. Windamere adds a northern character to the distinctive flavour of this southern coffee by hand-roasting the beans in a rotating drum over a very slow charcoal fire. The beans are then ground to perfection in an old-fashioned coffee mill just prior to brewing.

I read on, enchanted:

There may be occasional small variations with coffee brewed for you at meals. Coffee making, even now, remains more of an Art than a Science at Windamere.

There was more:

INFORMATION FOR NEW GUESTS
We have been filtering and boiling our drinking water since 1939. No one has been known to become ill after drinking our water. Nevertheless, if you prefer to drink mineral water, we keep an adequate supply in hand.

Mineral water, I quickly discerned, is the Windamere's sole concession to modernity. The hotel is run (I am assuming it is the same in 2002) on the principle that the Raj is still in existence, as I learned that first evening when I dined alone in the restaurant, the chalet adjacent to the house.

The cuisine, in 1994, was Anglo-Indian. The meal was of a memorable ghastliness, reminding me of the school dinners I'd had to endure forty years earlier. There was that clear soup, which might or might not have been Brown Windsor, to begin with, followed by an unidentifiable fish, accompanied by defrosted, lukewarm beans and carrots, and a chicken curry which contained the tiniest chicken leg I had ever seen, with barely a mouthful of flesh on it. The curry had a distinctly English look about it, since the powder was manufactured, not prepared in the kitchen. I declined the banana crumble, swamped in lumpy custard, and drank a cup of coffee made with Art rather than Science. It tasted disgusting.

I had noticed on entering the restaurant a tall woman with obviously dyed black hair who was swathed in a gaudy yellow and green evening dress. 'Are you by chance from England?' she enquired, in a very posh Kensington accent. I answered yes. 'From London?' Yes, again. 'Thank you,' she said, smiling mysteriously.

It transpired that there were five other English people staying at the hotel, and two of them were in the dining room. I suddenly heard 'Maybe it's Because I'm a Londoner' being played on an upright piano behind me. I turned round in my chair and saw that the pianist was the gaudily dressed woman I had just spoken to. She then gave a hearty rendition of 'I've Got a Lovely Bunch of Coconuts'. 'Roll Out the Barrel' and 'Two Lovely Black Eyes' came next. The two elderly Englishwomen opposite me were trying desperately to stifle their giggles, and so was I. The English music hall theme once exhausted, the pianist plunged into 'Santa Lucia' and 'Over the Rainbow'. The most enthusiastic member of her audience was a tiny old woman, sitting in state at the end of the room and beaming with pleasure. The waiters treated her with special attentiveness.

There were two hot water bottles in my bed and a coal fire, lit by a maid, was burning. I had to remind myself that the year was 1994, and that I was in India, not some chilly English suburb. My bedtime reading, with a glass of Indian brandy to hand, was the notes I had overlooked earlier:

About salads, all uncooked vegetables are washed thoroughly in 'pinki-pani', or potassium permanganate (the stuff you gargle with when you have a sore throat) before being served. We have been doing this also since 1939.

That particular note made the idea of ordering salad instantly resistible.

The next note exhorted:

SEND IT TO KAN-CHI

If you need a sock darned, a button sewn on, or a stitch put in a seam, please send the article for repair to Kan-Chi through your room maid. Kan-Chi sews for love. Her service is free.

There was a final note to study:

WINDERMERE [sic] TEA. Served by the fire, in the sitting-room of Windamere Hotel, since 1939. Remembered by guests as 'The Champagne of Teas'.

I began to realize 1939 was a key year in the Windamere's history.

I rose early the following morning, had a warmish shower, and went to the dining room for breakfast. I told the Nepalese waiter that I wanted very weak Darjeeling tea without milk or sugar, and I ordered scrambled eggs. I thought I was safe with scrambled eggs, but I was wrong. The tea was fine, but the eggs were grey, their greyness emphasized by the dollop of mashed potato that came with them. I remembered powdered egg from my childhood in wartime, and wondered if the chef was still using the supply the hotel had purchased in – could it be? – 1939.

I wandered about the town, taking in some long-in-the-tooth American disciples of Hare Krishna, passing the NU LADEE beauty parlour, and a little cinema that was showing FILTHY DELIGHT, with the unnecessary caution 'For Adults Only'. I found a bookshop that contained every book P. G.

Wodehouse had written – which seemed appropriate, since the great chronicler of English idiocy might have invented the Windamere. I visited a tea plantation, and bought various kinds of Darjeeling and Sikkim tea. The saddest sight was of a pair of abandoned ponies – too old and frail now to be of use. One of them followed me some of the way up Observatory Hill, until he was scared off by a troop of excited monkeys. Every litter bin on the hill had a message from the Darjeeling Council printed on it, my favourite being ALLOW US TO KEEP YOU SMILE. On my way to the zoo – where wonderfully beautiful Siberian and Indian tigers were kept in far too confined a space – I paused before the HOT AND STIMULATING CAFE, which specialized in tea and instant coffee (produced with Science, and probably tastier than the kind made with Art).

I was in Darjeeling, courtesy of the British Council, to talk to the teachers and students at Loreto College. I was immediately charmed by the principal, Reverend Mother Damien O'Donoghue, not least because she spoke about Shakespeare, Keats, Dickens and Jane Austen with luminous enthusiasm. It was clear that the staff and pupils respected and loved her. I spent two days at the college, and was impressed by the quality and intelligence of the questions I was asked. Of the teachers, I best remember a large man – the Nepalese and Sikkim are small in stature – whose eyes disappeared into his head whenever he spoke. I was so intrigued by this ocular vanishing trick that I scarcely heard what he was saying.

Mitalee joined me to savour the delights of Windamere cuisine: a cream of potato and onion soup, straight from the tin or packet, thick with monosodium glutamate; roast beef with Yorkshire pudding, potatoes and carrots, and a curry with pork and vegetables. Crème caramel was the dessert. Mitalee, being Hindu, refused the beef and I resisted the Yorkshire pudding, which resembled a dry biscuit. There was a power cut during the meal – the pianist played gamely on, by candlelight – so I escorted Mitalee to the New Elgin Hotel, and I, in turn, was guided back to the Windamere by a tiny man with a torch.

Guests can take afternoon tea in the sitting room, dominated by a picture of the youthful Elizabeth II, or in Daisy's Music Room. It was in the latter that I drank the 'Champagne of Teas' (not quite as terrible as the coffee made with Art) and then had a Bloody Mary. The pianist, playing on a slightly less tinny upright, entertained me with standards by Cole Porter, Gershwin, Jerome Kern and Noël Coward. As she tickled the ivories with her customary panache, I flicked through some of the many photograph albums on a side table. They dated back to 1912 – the year the chain-action water closets were installed. Daisy was the daughter of the original owner of Windamere, and can be seen kitted out for tennis or on a croquet lawn with her parents. The photos tell the story of the Raj in miniature – men in linen suits or in the uniform of their regiment; a whole ensemble of bored-looking women, their pearls on prominent display, daring the camera to conceal their boredom. Everybody dressed for dinner, and everyone got blotto (the *mot juste*) at Christmas, to judge by the expressions captured for posterity.

In 1994, the Windamere was ruled over by the beaming woman I had seen in the restaurant. She walked with the aid of a stick. The pianist told me that Madam, as she was addressed by the 'boys' and maids who worked there, was related to the Sikkim Royal Family. Madam came into Daisy's Music Room, mid-Gershwin, and said to the pianist, 'Tea in the private dining room at four tomorrow.' The musician was overcome. 'In the private dining room, Madam. What an honour.'

When her bravura performance was done, the pianist and I went out on to the terrace, with its breathtaking view of the Himalayas. 'I sigh for the old England,' she announced. She gasped for breath at the end of each sentence. 'No more lovely pounds, shillings and pence,' she boomed. 'Nothing but decimal, decimal.' Yes, she had lived in London, but not when the socialists were in power. And yes, she was Anglo-Indian, but with the emphasis very much on the Anglo. Would she go back to London? 'Good God, no. Not while Harrods is owned by an Arab.' I said how much I loved the music she had just been playing, and she observed that she was trying, with little success, to bring her repertoire up to date. 'There only seems to be Mr Lloyd Webber on the musical horizon.'

On my last morning, I ordered scrambled eggs again, hoping that something pleasingly yellow would appear on my plate. It was a vain hope. They were as grey as before, but there was no mashed potato. A curled-up strip of bacon, mostly fat, was the only accompaniment.

Mitalee came to the hotel for a farewell lunch. We were on the terrace when the pianist appeared, clutching a gin and tonic. 'Are you going to entertain us for lunch?' I asked. 'No, no, no,' she responded. 'I only do cocktails and dinner. If I did luncheon as well, I'd be *whacked*.'

We travelled back to the city of plump sacred cows and famished stray dogs, of vibrant life and reeking death, by overnight train. I was glad to be returning to the real world after my brief sojourn in that make-believe Raj, with its dreadful, ultra-English food, and those diminutive servants literally bowing and scraping.

Shortly before I checked out, I saw Madam talking to an American. I learned that he had married into her (royal) family and was now the proud owner of the Windamere. The myth of the undying Raj was being sustained from the other side of the Atlantic. Perhaps it still is, and no doubt the scrambled eggs are still grey.

I phoned Jeremy from Calcutta, telling him about the Windamere and its antiquated ways. And he assured me that Circe was in exuberant health, bothering the bewildered Max with her unsubtle advances.

Scrap

The house on the corner was owned for many years by a one-eyed Serb with a mouthful of metal teeth. Its occupants were notable for the pall of depression and failure that hung over them. They were men of all ages, each one of whom had a woefully familiar story to tell, if anyone had ever felt inclined to listen to it. They lived in the upper rooms, which were sparsely furnished – wardrobe, bed, table, chair – beneath a solitary light bulb dangling from the ceiling. They came and went, these drifters – some making their exit in the middle of the night; others dying on the premises or in the local hospitals. The house on the corner would have been the perfect setting for *The Lower Depths*, Maxim Gorky's play about the terminally dispossessed in a town in Tsarist Russia.

There was one regular tenant, who lived on the ground floor. Brian was very fat when I first saw him in the 1970s, but in two decades he grew to be enormous. He was a scrap merchant, dealing in anything discarded he could sell for a small profit. His lorry was often parked outside a nearby betting shop. I can't remember when he abandoned his profession, but it must have been towards the end of the 1980s, when the lorry became a permanent fixture yards from my front door. Brian was now too large to fit into the driver's seat, and the strain of adjusting his belly behind the wheel was making him angry and upset.

I looked out on that lorry for eighteen months. Passing

motorists used it as a rubbish tip. Its tyres began to sink into the road. I complained to an environment officer at Hammersmith Council, who advised me to consult the police. I rang the police, who suggested I complain to the council. I duly phoned the council again, and learned that the removal of the lorry was the responsibility of the police. I retired, bewildered.

Then, one afternoon, the Features Editor of the London *Evening Standard* called to ask me to write a column for the following day. I could choose any subject I wished. Thus it was that I penned a eulogy to Brian's lorry, with its array of rusty cookers, battered television sets, threadbare clothes and worn-out electric and gas fires. I loved the view from my window, I declared, for it reminded me of the vanity of human aspirations and the transient nature of modern technology. I thanked the council and the police for their splendid obtuseness, for without their indifference I should have been deprived of the melancholy vision I delighted in each passing day.

My heavy-handed irony must have irritated someone in authority, for I awoke the very next morning to see the lorry being tugged away. Such, I told myself, is the power of the printed word.

As he became fatter and fatter, Brian developed into a philosopher. He would hold court from a wobbly chair on the doorstep, expressing opinions he had read in the editorial page of the *Sun*, his favourite newspaper. He usually had a couple of cronies to sound off to before drink made them incoherent or incapable of listening, or both. He cursed me, playfully, as a wishy-washy liberal, though he always praised Circe's beauty and envied her slimness. Whenever I returned from Romania,

I brought him back a gallon of *ţuica*, the lethal plum or apricot brandy I find undrinkable.

Brian died in his sleep, and the one-eyed Serb sold the filthy dosshouse to a man who, after two dedicated years, has transformed it into something palatial. Gorky's desperate waifs and strays would not feel at home in it.

Circe and Cleopatra

In 1995 I decided that I wanted to learn Romanian. I also decided that I needed a teacher. I already knew a few basic words and had followed a course on two cassettes, but now I needed to be guided through the language's tortuous grammar. I phoned an acquaintance at the Romanian Embassy, asking for help. There was a student at the School of Slavonic and East European Studies in the University of London who might be interested in giving me lessons, she said. She would make enquiries on my behalf.

My tutor turned out to be a beautiful, raven-haired young woman called Cleopatra. Was Cleopatra a common name in Romania? 'No, no, no,' she laughed. 'It was my mother's idea. I prefer that you call me Cleo.' The shortened version, she added, was less of an embarrassment to her.

She came to the house every Wednesday afternoon for several months. We worked at the kitchen table, with Circe – who approved of her – sometimes curled at her feet. She often brought newspaper or magazine articles for me to translate into English. With the aid of *A Course in Contemporary Romanian*, I managed to construct sentences that sounded as if they hadn't come out of a phrase book. She was patient when I committed ludicrous errors, and praising on those occasions when I saw chinks of light in the linguistic darkness.

★

Early in 1989, I received a letter from the Literature Department of the British Council inviting me to visit Romania. I accepted the invitation and flew to Bucharest on a fine Sunday in March, having first deposited Circe at the kennels Michael Gordon had recommended, and where she was known as by far the most voluble and certainly the most energetic of all the dogs the staff had ever cared for.

I set off in more or less total ignorance of the country and its customs. I had no idea, then, that the language would be so approachable and so appealing to the ear. And although I was aware that Romania was currently in the hands of a dictator named Nicolae Ceauşescu, I had no knowledge of the extent of his wickedness. He and his wife, Elena, had been in England in the 1970s, courtesy of the Prime Minister, James Callaghan. The bizarre, diminutive couple had stayed in Buckingham Palace, and the Queen had bestowed upon him the oldest and highest honour in Britain, the Order of the Garter. That much – or rather, that little – I knew.

I was met at the airport by a young man in a long black leather coat who informed me that I was the guest of the Romanian Writers' Union. As the week progressed, I began to wonder what crime I had perpetrated in order to attain this dubious honour. The young man told me he was a television playwright. I was not immediately suspicious of this claim since I understood nothing at that time of the curious workings of Romanian television. I would soon discover by switching on the TV in my hotel bedroom that the screen was blank for most of the day, only coming to dreary life at four in the afternoon with the transmission of parliamentary proceedings. I watched Ceauşescu as he droned on and on from the podium for the regulated two hours. Every ten minutes

or so, the toadies in the hall afforded him a standing ova-
tion, as if on cue. Here was television drama of a sickening,
soporific kind.

The Writers' Union had booked me into an expensive
hotel on the Calea Victoriei – the Street of Victories. A surly
individual – the first of many thugs I was to encounter – gave
me a form to complete. The playwright assisted me. I was
asked to give my father's date of birth. My father sired me
when he was on the brink of old age, dying when I was very
young. I had forgotten when he was born, but I guessed it
had to be in the 1880s. I wrote 20 April 1888, and the surly
receptionist, reading it, looked up and eyed me with contemptuous disbelief. I have always looked younger than my
years, and in 1989 I could have passed for someone in his late
thirties or early forties. The man with the fixed sneer clearly
thought I was having a complicated joke at his expense. It was
something to which he wasn't accustomed.

I was due to meet my interpreter, Lydia, the following
morning at nine o'clock. I rose at seven, had breakfast – the
waiter, who spoke perfect English, said he was a professional
actor – and decided to go for a walk. No sooner had I left the
hotel than two tall men in long black leather coats began to
trail me. I am in a spy novel, I thought as I pretended not to
notice them. There was a side street leading off the square I
had wandered into and I chose to run down it to give them
the slip. They ran after me, at a discreet pace. I was amused,
not frightened. I stopped in front of a bookshop, which was
already open. I walked in, and discovered within minutes that
all the books on offer were the Collected Speeches of Nicolae
Ceauşescu in virtually every language. This was vanity publishing on an unprecented scale. His thoughts, such as they

were, could be studied in Bengali, in Sanskrit, in Japanese, as well as in English, French, German and Italian. My leather-coated admirers, protectors – or even, perhaps, assassins – were making a great show of being fascinated by the window display. They kept a few paces behind me as I strolled back to the hotel.

The first thing that Lydia did was to stop me giving money to a gypsy child with an outstretched hand. I met several intellectuals that week, who spoke movingly and illuminatingly about Romania's terrible misfortunes, whenever they were at a safe distance from a bugging device. On the subject of the gypsies, however, they were almost unanimously hostile. The terminology of racial hatred is unvarying, wherever it's employed. I'd heard it in childhood when every landlord was called 'Shylock', and in my youth with the arrival of the 'darkies' in my native south London. But what I was hearing now, and wishing I wasn't – to the effect that the gypsies were 'taking the food out of the mouths of decent Romanians' – differed in one crucial respect. The predictable opinions were issuing from the mouths of people with university degrees, not the uneducated working-class men and women I grew up amongst. The odious villains in power suddenly seemed less responsible for the country's ills than those Romany scapegoats whose music inspired Bartók, who was born on what is now Romanian soil.

As we drove through the city in Lydia's tiny, and ubiquitous, Dacia, we passed shops selling cheap cuts of meat or stale bread, outside which long and apparently silent queues had formed. It was a dispiriting sight and one which I shall never forget. When we arrived at the Writers' Union headquarters, we were greeted by the palest man in the world, whose clothes matched his complexion in paleness. He offered us wine and announced that there was a choice of fish (carp) or chicken for lunch. Writers, I realized, were privileged in this culture, especially if they chose not to criticize the regime. They had husbands, wives and children to consider. I had to ask myself if I would have become a time-server had I been living under a dictatorship. I hoped not. I settled for the chicken.

On Tuesday morning I attempted to check out of the hotel. I had consumed two bottles of mineral water in my room, and tried to pay for them with Romanian money, of which I had been given an abundance. The surly receptionist would only accept American dollars, Deutschmarks or sterling. He threw the *lei* back at me as if they were dirt. I offered him my credit card. It was at this point the manager appeared, giving me back my card and assuring me that the water was free. I smiled at my enemy, who glowered.

I flew with Lydia to Suceava, where we were met by a uniformed chauffeur who led us to a government limousine. I was being given the VIP treatment. Lydia warned me not to say anything controversial in the car, because it was certain to be bugged. We passed through villages that Ceauşescu was currently intent on destroying, replacing them with what might be deemed housing estates. Peasants and farmhands stopped and stared as the vast black car – a hated symbol of authority – made its progress along bumpy country roads. We were going to see some of the undoubted marvels of Romanian art – the painted churches of Moldavia. The frescoes, depicting scenes from the life of Christ and his inevitable Passion, are on the outside of the churches and are in a state of almost miraculous preservation. As I stood in wonder, a troop of white ducks waddled past – the same white ducks who were accompanying Christ on the Via Dolorosa in the marvellous fresco, painted by anonymous hands, I was admiring.

The next stop was Iaşi, the capital of Moldavia, where 10,000 Jews were massacred in 1941. I was supposed to give a talk at the university, but this had been cancelled. (On governmental instructions, no less, I was to learn.) I spent the evening with Ştefan, an expert on American literature, and we got happily sozzled in a nearby restaurant thanks to the piles of *lei* I was carrying.

On Thursday morning I was in Bucharest again, and the surly receptionist was again on duty. He handed me the form to fill in. I reminded him that I had completed it on Sunday. He insisted that I do so once more. I remembered that my father's supposed date of birth was 20 April 1888, and duly recorded it. My dedicated foe seized the paper from me, but his hopes of chancing on a different date were confounded. I was all smiles.

That Friday was memorable in many ways. In the morning, the British Foreign Secretary, Sir Geoffrey Howe, condemned Romania's bad record on human rights. Dozens of writers and artists who had been invited to meet me at a reception in the British Embassy that evening were suddenly disinvited by telephone. I spent the morning with two translators and my future Romanian publisher, and was picked up by the television dramatist who drove me to the University of Bucharest. On the way, I asked him if there was a gay scene in the capital.

'By "gay" do you mean "humorous"?' he replied.

I told him what I meant.

'We do not have such people in Romania.'

'There must be some in Central and Eastern Europe,' I suggested.

'They are all in Budapest.'

He dropped me by the steps of the university and zoomed off. On arrival at the English department, I informed a woman who is now a friend and likes to be addressed as Micky, that I had come to give a talk to the students. 'But we were expecting you last Tuesday,' she said. She made me a cup of tea, then phoned the head of the department, who had gone home for the weekend. The two resourceful teachers rustled up about a hundred students, who plied me with questions on any number of subjects. The authorities had given the department the wrong day for my lecture, knowing perfectly well that I would be out of town. Micky and her boss were breaking the law by allowing me to speak on the Friday. They had no written permission to invite a visitor from abroad into the English department, even though the visitor was English. They knew they were taking a serious risk.

There were police cars galore in the streets surrounding the British Embassy. Mrs Arbuthnot, the wife of the ambassador, was laughing at the thought that a mere writer should attract more policemen than she had ever seen. The palest man in the world was at the party. 'What a pity you couldn't talk to the students today,' were his first words to me. The plot was unravelling. 'Oh, but I did,' I answered, and I swear he turned paler. 'What did you talk about?' he enquired when he had recovered somewhat from the shock. 'Lots of things,' I said. 'Politics, the theatre, sex.' 'How many students were there?' he asked, thinking of those young minds being tainted by Western decadence. 'A hundred. Perhaps more.'

As he walked away, Rosemary – who worked for the British Council, and spoke fluent, idiomatic Romanian – remarked of the world's palest man, 'He's such a wanker.' Hearing this,

Mrs Arbuthnot laughed even louder. 'Every room in this building is bugged,' she explained. 'I can just see them rushing to the *Oxford English Dictionary* to look up that word. You've really put them in a tizzy.'

After the reception, I went back to the flat Rosemary rented. There were five of us – a Romanian actor and his girlfriend, and a dissident poet whose hangdog expression haunted me for years. Nearly a decade later, I learned that he had been blackmailed into working for the Securitate, the secret police. A police car followed the taxi we were in, and remained outside the apartment until three in the morning. It followed me back to the hotel.

I checked out of the Intercontinental on Sunday morning. I thanked the surly receptionist for his interesting contribution to my happy stay. Rosemary came with me to the airport. A police car was again in attendance.

I was reunited with Circe on Monday. She was stand-offish for the first few minutes, reminding me with her soulful eyes that I had abandoned her. We were barely home before she was barking to go to the park. I obeyed her loud commands, and was eventually forgiven.

One of my new friends had related a wonderfully funny and sinister story during that eventful, surreal week. It seemed that a British politician, David Steel, had presented the Ceauşescus with a black Labrador puppy named Winston. Once in Romania, the dog was renamed Comrade Corbul ('corb' means 'raven', and can mean 'vulture') and made a member of the Communist party. He grew into a sleek and lively animal, because of the varied diet on which he was reared. No cheap cuts for him. My friend was waiting at the traffic lights on Calea Victoriei when a state limousine drew up in front of him. A uniformed chauffeur was, as ever, in the front seat, but it was the figure on the back seat that startled him. There was Comrade Corbul, with a ribboned medal on his chest, perched in lonely splendour, the grandest of political animals. 'I laughed at the sight, but then I choked on my laughter.'

In September 1989, I gave a dinner party for Antoinette Ralian, who had been granted a visa to study at the Bodleian in Oxford. She was Iris Murdoch's translator, and had also translated D. H. Lawrence. Under the Ceauşescus, the sexual act was outlawed in literature (the rampant Elena, who had her pick of the bodyguards, didn't like to think of others enjoying themselves) and Antoinette had serious problems rendering the wrestling scene in *Women in Love* into allusive Romanian. Over dinner, we talked of the liberty such countries as Hungary and Poland were about to achieve, and Antoinette became tearful. 'It could never happen in Romania,' she sighed.

But it could, and it did, after a terrible fashion, that very Christmas, when the crowds in Timişoara and Bucharest defied the police and the army and heckled the perplexed dictator as he tried, and failed, to placate his once docile and frightened people from the balcony of the parliament building. Elena and Nicolae went into hiding, but were captured, put on farcical trial, and shot. One of their self-appointed 'judges' would kill himself two months later.

It was then that something of the corruption and wickedness that had prevailed in Romania for more than a decade was revealed to the civilized world. The orphanages into which AIDS-infected and unwanted children had been dumped and the mental institutions where rational dissidents were receiving 'treatment' were opened up for inspection. These horrors were unique to Romania. Elsewhere in the Eastern bloc, those defying the status quo were sentenced to imprisonment. The idea of the insane asylum as a place of detention, where the disease of speaking the truth can be diagnosed and cured, is entirely fitting for the culture that produced Dadaism and the absurdist drama of Eugène Ionesco.

After that hectic week in March 1989, I decided that Ionesco, far from being an absurdist, was in fact a realist. Plays like *The Chairs* and, especially, *Rhinoceros* presage the nightmares and deceits of Ceauşescu's Romania. I reread Ionesco with a renewed sense of his brilliance and prescience. I recalled how the theatre critic Kenneth Tynan, posing as a committed socialist, attacked the dramatist for being apolitical, taking him to flippant task for his pessimism. Yet it's Ionesco who endures, and his refusal to espouse the immovable doctrines of Right and Left seems wholly humane in the context of Romanian history from 1930 to 1989. And, alas, beyond.

I returned to Bucharest in the winter of 1992, the third anniversary of the so-called revolution. I write 'so-called' because that's the expression everyone I met was using. No one believed that it was a genuine uprising. There were rumours that the protests in Timişoara had been master-minded by the Russians and the downfall of the latterday Macbeths planned within the party. It was viciously cold in the city, and although there was inviting and nutritious food in the shops only a tiny minority could afford the luxury of smoked salmon or fillet steak or *noisettes* of lamb. The books were different, too. In the Communist era it was impossible to buy unashamedly popular fiction, but now the works of Jackie Collins, Barbara Cartland, Jack Higgins and Danielle Steel, among others, were there beside the established classics. During my visit, Antoinette was busy translating a novel by someone called Sandra Brown (a name of such ordinariness that it has to be made up) for one of the new commercial publishing houses that had appeared almost overnight in January 1990. She was earning more money than she had ever been paid by the official state publishers, but at a spiritual cost. 'There aren't too many ways of saying "fuck" in Romanian,' she observed sadly.

(The two Romanian–English dictionaries in my possession were published while Ceauşescu was in power. There are no definitions for 'penis', 'testicles', 'vagina', 'clitoris' or 'homosexual'. The cruder variants are, naturally, absent. Romania was a pure country and its language similarly immaculate and untainted by carnality.)

That December I stayed in a run-down, but once opulent, hotel. A group of Sicilians who had boarded the connecting flight at Zürich were also staying there. They wore striped suits, two-toned shoes and fedoras – a clichéd combination that shrieked out MAFIA. They did business in the hotel lobby. A friend, calling on me, noticed two of them in earnest conversation with a member of the government. There were armed guards in the lobby all day and night, and at six every evening the prostitutes – some in fur coats because of the weather – arrived for work. They looked fit and well-fed, unlike the wasted boys and girls who were attempting to sell their bodies at the Gare du Nord, the central railway station. Like Jo the crossing-sweeper in *Bleak House*, they were subsequently 'moved on' – to die out of sight, presumably. They were distressing the tourists with their bulging eyes and skeletal frames: the awful evidence of the AIDS-related illnesses they were suffering.

A whole community of lost and abandoned children was

living in the city's sewers, I learned. Several of these waifs had died the same gruesome death. Overcome by hunger and the need to steal or beg for something to eat, they would emerge from an uplifted manhole and get run over by a car or truck. Since their lives were worthless anyway, and their place of residence illegal, it was generally considered that they were responsible for their own demise. If you ignore the circumstances that led them to the sewers, that point of view makes sense. The drivers were victims, not killers.

I contacted the British Council during my trip and, hearing that George, the Council's driver, was going to Iaşi, I asked if he could give me a lift in the Land Rover. It was on that long ride across the snow-covered countryside that I made my first serious acquaintance with the language. Andy, a librarian, whose Romanian parents had been English teachers in Rhodesia, taught me the words for the birds and objects we saw on the journey – *coţofana*, magpie, being the first. The ebullient George was my delighted tutor as well, of a much more basic vocabulary, which includes *labagiu*, the Romanian for the term Rosemary used to describe the palest man in the world.

I had dinner with Ştefan in Iaşi and another man, a lecturer at the university, joined us. He was tipsy on arrival, and got drunker and drunker as the meal progressed. He revealed, for my benefit I assumed, that he lived in domestic misery, with a wife and daughter who both hated him. It turned out that the house in which I was spending the night was next to his own, so we shared a taxi late in the evening. He had heard me reading from my memoir *An Immaculate Mistake* in Cambridge in 1990 and told me how brave I was to be so open about my homosexuality. Such courage was impossible and unthinkable in Romania, he said. As soon as we were out of the taxi, he made a lunge in my direction, trying to kiss me on the lips. I managed to push him off and say I wasn't interested. Once inside the house, I discovered there was no key to the lock on my bedroom door. So, absurdly, I secured a chair beneath the door handle, to fend off the bear-like individual who had designs on me. There I was, at the age of fifty-three, behaving as if I were some timid virgin. I could laugh about it in the morning, but I had been scared. I mentioned the incident to Ştefan, who was not surprised. The Securitate had discovered that the man was homosexual many years ago and had threatened him with imprisonment and worse if he didn't cooperate. They advised him to marry, to ensure that his secret never became common knowledge. The lecturer had been informing on his colleagues for three decades, at least. He was not happy in this task, as his often excessive drinking indicated.

The lecturer's predicament was not an isolated one. Thousands of people were caught in the Securitate's wide-ranging trap. In that pure Romania, even the slightest sexual peccadillo could lead to blackmail and humiliation by the police. That notion of a national purity hasn't died with Communism. It is currently espoused by Corneliu Vadim Tudor, the leader of the Far Right opposition party. As if to emphasize the pure nature of the Romanian soul, Tudor always appears in public dressed in white – white suit, white shirt or sweater, white socks, white shoes. Garbed as a wingless angel, Tudor denounces Jews (not many of them left in the Balkans), Gypsies, Turks, and indeed all foreigners.

When the television playwright gave outraged expression to 'We do not have such people in Romania' he was honouring a dictate from on high. In that iniquitous society it was essential to remind the average men and women of Romania's moral superiority in an otherwise immoral Europe. This imposed belief had its uses, not least the idea that financial prosperity is the root cause of decadence. Tell that to the poor as they wait in line for meat or bread. If 'decadent' is defined as 'characterized by decay or decline', then Romania is the most decadent country I have ever visited. And that is part of its fascination for me.

Throughout my first trip to Romania, there was a curfew every evening from seven-thirty onwards. Theatrical performances began at around five o'clock. I remember a production of *The Taming of the Shrew* which reduced the packed audience to helpless laughter. I have never regarded the play as particularly funny, so I asked Rosemary, who was sitting beside me, why everyone was laughing. She replied that the actors were improvising when they saw fit, sneaking in sarcastic asides that clearly referred to their hated leader and his unlovely spouse. There must have been a surfeit of these asides for the laughter, often accompanied by spontaneous applause, was fairly constant.

In December 1999, the theatres opened at seven or eight. I sat through a performance of *Richard III*, starring a mesmeric actor named Marcel Iureş, that almost made me forget I was freezing. There was no heating in the theatre, and no bar either. The apartments of friends were similarly chilly, with everybody present huddled around a single electric fire or oil-fuelled stove that gave out very little heat.

The wide Bucharest streets were filthy and pitted with holes. The vast palace, larger than Versailles, that Ceauşescu had built to his own glory, stood unoccupied. I had been granted a tour of the monstrous piece of kitsch as an honoured guest of the Writers' Union. Sceptics, in unbugged open spaces, had revealed that whole areas of the city had been felled to accommodate Ceauşescu's folly and the long avenue leading up to it. It wasn't only houses and business premises and hotels that were destroyed. Orthodox churches disappeared, too, and an irreplaceable, centuries-old mosque.

The antique shops in the wealthy heart of Bucharest were selling icons – some of considerable beauty – in their hundreds. Where had they come from? The answer was as simple as it was painful. The icons had been owned, and hidden, by devout families, who had prayed before them over many generations. They were on sale now, at exorbitant prices, because their former owners had to eat and needed money to do so. The dealers bought the icons from these newly impoverished men and women – who used to be able to afford cheap cuts and stale bread – for risibly small amounts of *lei*. The icons were not on sale in Romanian currency, of course. I picked up a tiny icon of St Nicholas that appealed to me and wondered what it cost. On hearing that I could have it for three thousand American dollars, I suddenly decided it didn't appeal to me that much.

There were other, visible casualties of the country's surreal economy, in the pathetic shape of the stray dogs who were roaming the icy city in search of scraps. They couldn't be sold, like the icons, merely abandoned. The one-time pets had become too expensive to support and had been thrown out or dumped from cars to fend for themselves. I thought of Circe, at home in London in Jeremy's fond care, as yet another mangy, half-starved dog limped or padded past.

It had been impossible during the Communist years to buy

bananas in Romania. Only the older people – and those who had been allowed out of the country – remembered their appearance and taste. The arrival of the banana early in 1990 inspired a joke I heard many times. It runs like this: One thing has changed in Bucharest, and one thing hasn't. You can now buy bananas, but the trams are still full to overflowing. A man purchases three loose bananas – one for him, one for his wife, and one for his son. He has to travel home by tram and is worried that the precious fruit will be squashed. He places a banana in each of the side pockets of his jacket and the third in the back pocket of his trousers. He boards the tram, and very soon he is surrounded by fellow passengers, jammed tight against them. He realizes his already ripe bananas are suffering the fate he anticipated, and puts his hand behind him to test the condition of the one in his back pocket. To his relief, he finds it reassuringly hard, and decides to keep a firm grip on it for the rest of the journey. Many stops later, he feels a pat on his shoulder and turns his head to see a man smiling at him. The man says, very politely, 'Excuse me, but do you think you could let go of my penis? I have to get off here.'

As I watched an ancient episode of *Dallas* in my hotel room, I felt curious to know how the television playwright was faring. The next day I enquired after him and received a derisive guffaw as response. I learned that he'd worked for the Securitate and was no longer around. His skills as a dramatist had yet to be tested.

I immersed myself, as best I could in London, in Romanian culture and history. Kitty's father had worked for Shell in Romania from 1946 to 1948, when the country became part of the Soviet bloc, and she gave me some of his books after his death. Among these is the only English translation of Ion Creanga's *Recollections*, published in 1930. This memoir, and the wonderful fairy tales that accompany it, appeared in 1890 and 1892, and is regarded as the first substantial prose work in the language. (It is important to understand that there was no *written* Romanian until the early years of the nineteenth century.) *Recollections* describes what it was like to grow up in a Moldavian peasant family in a superstitious society totally cut off from the changing world. Such communities, smaller in number, continue to exist in the more remote areas of the countryside.

I read R. W. Seton-Watson's magisterial *A History of the Roumanians*, in which I encountered such diverse, and blood-thirsty, national heroes as Vlad the Impaler, Michael the Brave and Romania's very own Peter the Great. But it is *Athene Palace* by Countess Waldeck – an American journalist despite the title – that offers the most acute insights into the Romanian character. She stayed in the hotel (its proper name is Athénée) from the summer of 1940 until the end of January 1941, when the Germans were dictating every move of General Anton-escu's government. She watched its capitulation to the Nazis from a position of privilege, having befriended every important person in the capital, including a pair of priapic old aristocrats – one resembling a 'sick greyhound' – who primed her with gossip both sexual and political. It's the greyhound who con-fesses that, although he is anti-Semitic, he would rather do business with Jews because 'no Romanian trusts another Romanian'.

A passage in the epilogue of *Athene Palace* strikes me as especially perceptive:

I left the Athene Palace at the end of January 1941, knowing that Germany's bloodless conquest of Romania was as complete as if her armies had trampled the land underfoot and her airplanes bombarded the cities from the skies . . . Here nobody complained about the 'end of civilization' just because Hitler tried to set up a mere one-thousand-year Empire. A people that saw the Roman Empire come and go and saw all sorts of barbarians invade their country, and still survived, does not believe there is a definite end to anything. Such people are instinctively wise in the strange ways of history, which invariably seems to run into compromise, and so they are less afraid than many great nations of the West. The Romanians possess to the highest degree the capacity of receiving the blows of destiny while relaxed. They fall artfully, soft and loose in every joint and muscle as only those trained in falling can be. The secret of the art of falling is, of course, not to be afraid of falling and the Romanians are not afraid, as Western people are. Long experience in survival has taught them that each fall may result in unforeseen opportunities and that somehow they always get on their feet again.

Under Cleo's patient tutelage I began to understand Romanian grammar. *A Course in Contemporary Romanian* also contains, besides the inevitable lists of nouns and verbs and advice on how to employ them correctly, a selection of poems by the greatest Romanian poets. Thus it was that I discovered Mihai Eminescu, the great Romantic who is regarded as his country's Keats, and George Bacovia, the melancholy genius whose life was plagued by drink, depression and bouts of madness, but whose poetry has an eerie radiance.

At school in the 1950s, my English teachers had encouraged me to learn poems by heart. It has been a lifelong practice.

With Cleo to correct and improve my pronunciation, I committed one of Eminescu's poems to memory. 'Peste Vîrfurí' (O'er the Treetops) has the poet hearing the sound of a distant horn in the woods where the alder trees are shaking in the evening breeze. The moon appears and the sound fades away and he thinks of soothing death.

In 1996, I returned to Romania with a group of writers. On the first day I attended a reception in a Bucharest bookshop to celebrate the publication of two of my novels. Cleopatra's mother was there, and I told her how much I liked her beautiful daughter. A Romanian friend, Irina, asked me to recite 'Peste Vîrfurí', which I did. My brief recitation made front page news the next morning. I love the absurdity of it, and a certain sweetness. An Englishman reciting a masterpiece by the national poet seemed to assume more importance than murder or politics. Romanians are overjoyed when foreigners exhibit an interest in their literature – which is little translated, and mostly unknown abroad.

In Oradea, near the Hungarian border, the mayor welcomed the British and Romanian writers who had come to take part in a three-day seminar. Among those writers was the novelist Jonathan Coe. The mayor had no trouble with 'Jonathan', but 'Coe' confused him. He hesitated, and then pronounced it 'Coaie', to hoots of laughter from all the Romanians. 'Coaie' means 'balls'.

On that trip, my publisher, Denisa, gave me a copy of the complete works of Bacovia. It's a treasured book. On those mornings when I was alone in the park with Circe I would mutter his poems under my breath as I threw the ball for her.

Cleo went back to Bucharest, where she found a job with an American company. She is married now, and hopes to emigrate to Canada with her husband. She sees no future in Romania, which Bacovia encompasses in the exquisite line *O, ţară tristă, plină de humor.* 'O, sad country, full of humour.'

Raskolnikov

I called him Raskolnikov, after the would-be Superman turned repentant murderer in Dostoevsky's *Crime and Punishment*. He was tall and pale, with lank hair and a black beard. He wore a long black overcoat with black trousers and black shoes that had flapping soles. His white shirt was collarless, in the Russian style.

From a short distance, he looked anguished, his burning dark eyes signalling pain fiercely borne. 'It's Raskolnikov to the life,' I caught myself muttering the first time I saw him coming towards me on Uxbridge Road. I knew I stared at him in amazement. Then, as he passed me and the dog, he began to sing, in a very loud and effeminate voice:

Step inside, love,
Let me find you a place

and stopped abruptly, his frail body shaking with laughter.

I passed him often that year. He seemed to live on the streets of west London, this vision of blackness and spiritual torment with a passion for a song by Paul McCartney. I sighted him once in the park as he walked determinedly across the grass, laughing fiendishly.

On those many occasions when our paths crossed, he sang the opening bars of 'Step Inside, Love' before the terrible hilarity of his predicament took hold of him. Did he sing only for me, I wondered? Had he detected a kindred, appreciative spirit in the blatantly staring man with the friendly dog? Our lives are composed in part each day of questions that can never be answered.

The singing Raskolnikov became more and more wasted, lost inside the overcoat he wrapped around him tightly when he burst into song. I noticed him one hot afternoon biting into a hamburger with the ferocity of a wild animal. The meat was spilling out of his mouth and on to his glistening beard.

His truncated rendering of 'Step Inside, Love' on the last morning we passed one another was as manic as ever. His eyes, I imagined, were fixed on the death that was obviously awaiting him, just as the inevitable braying laugh was meant for the Grim Reaper. London's bustling Uxbridge Road – with its population of Serbs, Croats, Poles, Turks, Indians, Arabs and Armenians – was now his Styx, and his expected Charon was around the corner, ready to ferry him across. He was openly dying, with a forced, final energy.

Raskolnikov had been a pretty youth, I learned, but when I encountered him he was already suffering from an AIDS-related illness. Other people, I discovered, thought he resembled Jesus Christ. Yet I was in the habit of calling him Raskolnikov, and so he remains for me.

Roman Artichokes

Some years ago I was invited to review a book by the Chilean novelist Isabel Allende about the aphrodisiac qualities of everyday food. The mistress of hothouse prose was writing from personal experience – every recipe had been kitchen-tested, so to speak – when she informed her panting readership that even the humblest vegetable has powers to excite the jaded or worn-out libido. The potency of the potato – the prime source of vodka – was no surprise to me, and I could accept that the guava and the avocado pear have properties that might lead the unwary up otherwise ignored garden paths. But it was her gushing recommendation of the globe artichoke that disconcerted me, and called to mind an unforgettable evening in Rome – a windy evening, with a windier night to follow.

I had been commissioned to write and present a radio documentary about the life and work of Leonardo Sciascia, the great Sicilian writer who had died the previous year. Just before leaving for Palermo, via Rome, I had broken my tibia (a bone above the ankle) while running alongside Circe in the park. As a consequence, my right leg was in plaster and I could walk only with the aid of crutches. Jeremy accompanied me. We were making our way to the taxi rank at Rome airport when two nuns passed us at a gallop, one of them stopping briefly to trip me up with her black-booted right foot. I fell to the ground, shouting '*Fica*' after her. Roman nuns are a curiously charmless bunch, but I had never anticipated that they would stoop to injuring a cripple. Perhaps, I wondered later, the loathsome duo were *mafiosi* in drag. It's hard to tell what sex they are at times, since nuns in the Italian south are very circumspect when it comes to taking a razor to their facial hair. The husband of these brides of Christ is full of advice on other, more spiritual, concerns, but he seldom counsels them to have a shave.

We were in Rome for a couple of days, during which I interviewed Francesco Rosi, whose fine, intelligent movies – *Salvatore Giuliano*, which deals with the doomed life of the legendary Sicilian bandit, and *La Tregua* (The Truce), based on Primo Levi's account of his flight from Auschwitz – are little known outside his own country. We spent a day in Ravello, where I talked to Gore Vidal in the garden of his luxurious villa. Seeing me hobbling towards him, he exclaimed, 'Don't tell me. You gave Joyce Carol Oates a bad review, and she threw the full weight of her a hundred and ten pounds on to you.' He talked lyrically about Sciascia for more than an hour, without remembering a single title of his many books. Earlier that autumn afternoon, Jeremy and I and the producer of the programme, Noah Richler, had lunch at the wonderful little restaurant Cumpa Cosima, owned and managed by the enchanting Signora Netta, whom I had met some years before when Vanni and I had dined at Cumpa Cosima every night for a week. On returning to London, I wrote an article for the *Daily Telegraph* in which I described the food – the succulent roast lamb; the exquisite *crespellini*, which are pancakes filled with spinach – and lauded the unbelievably modest cost of everything on the carefully balanced menu. As a result, well-heeled British tourists, resident for the summer in places like

Positano, negotiated the dangerously narrow roads leading up to Ravello from Amalfi in their hired cars in order to eat well and save money. And now, serving us lunch, Netta thanked me profusely and pointed to my article, which was on the wall, behind glass and framed. The meal was on the house, and we left in a glow, promising to return.

Our time in Palermo was memorable for three things. On the first evening, Jeremy, Noah and I went by taxi to dine at a restaurant a knowledgeable Italian friend had recommended. The driver seemed loath to enter the *piazza* I had asked him to take us to, and we soon learned the reason for his apprehensiveness. As he drove into the square, the door of the restaurant flew open and a man rushed out, followed by another who shot him at close range. The taxi driver backed his vehicle out of danger with astonishing speed, and the three of us enjoyed ourselves at a quieter establishment.

It was while Noah and I were wandering around the Public Record Office – a favourite haunt of Sciascia's – that I noticed a cat making a path through the piles of yellowed ledgers that were scattered over the floor. (The shelves had been groaningly full for decades.) 'What's the cat for?' I enquired of the curator, who replied, matter-of-factly, 'To kill the mice and rats who destroy these precious documents.' The history of Palermo, I realized, is there for rodents to devour, and future historians of the city would have to thank a scraggy tabby (and his successors) for preserving it from their nibbling molars.

A visit to the Catacombs proved too discomfiting for Noah, who retreated in horror from the sight of so many skulls and bones. Jeremy and I revelled in this macabre spectacle of human vanity, with its foolish desire to outwit death. The skeletons were arranged in different sections, each relating to their owners' lifetime occupations: an old sailor, in the cellar devoted to naval and military heroes, was still wearing his three-cornered hat, while a soldier – whose uniform had all but evaporated – had a skeletal hand on a fellow soldier's skeletal knee. By design, or accident? We strolled past doctors, lawyers, politicians, actors and actresses, opera singers and erstwhile courtesans. Their clothes – some of them dating back to the early eighteenth century – were in various stages of decay and mildew. The one truly grisly corpse was, in fact, the most recent – that of a child who had been deposited in the Catacombs in the 1920s. She was the last resident, kept in a glass case. She had obviously been pumped up with embalming fluid, given the redness of her cheeks. Among the dead on display, she alone looked *living*.

Jeremy and I returned to Rome, to the beautiful Hotel Forum, in which we had stayed after my mugging by the nun. We were offered the bridal suite at a reduced price. The staff took my crippled state into consideration, for they treated us with charming solicitousness. That evening we decided to eat at a nearby *trattoria*, where the head waiter persuaded us to try the chicken breasts with artichokes. We expressed our delight with his recommendation.

In the vast double bed in the bridal suite, we settled down to sleep. Who was the first to break wind? I can't recall, but a duet of farts began at around midnight and kept us awake for hours. They were loud and cacophonous, and the odours they emanated caused us to lift the top sheet and employ it as a fan. They would stop for a while, only to recommence. We turned up the volume on the television, to drown the noises the delicious globe artichokes had induced.

It was the memory of that happy experience – for each new fart had us convulsed with incredulous laughter – that made me doubt the authenticity of Isabel Allende's treatise. Was this one recipe the dedicated researcher had overlooked? Or does she know of people for whom the mutual breaking of wind is a required accompaniment to sexual satisfaction? These questions continue to worry me, for unless I encounter Allende and confront her with them, they seem fated to remain unanswered.

Sisters

Trixie – or was it Tricksy? – was one of Circe's frequent companions. She was two-thirds lurcher and, in her active youth, sprang rather than ran across the park. She belonged to Daphne and her older sister Florence, who was known solely as Sis. The women owned a fruit-and-vegetable shop which they had inherited from their parents. When I first arrived in Shepherd's Bush in the early 1970s, their mother, Winifred, was still alive. Indifferent to the twentieth century, she drove to the market twice a week by horse and cart. She wore a broad-brimmed hat with a large pin stuck through it at all times, and looked the most forbidding of matriarchs as she urged the faithful old dobbin along or ordered her doting daughters to serve the customers.

After the horse's demise, a van was bought for Sis to drive. Winifred 'passed over' – to use, as Sis and Daphne used, that common euphemism for 'died'. Daphne was now in charge of the shop, while Sis pottered about in the kitchen behind it. (There was a perpetual smell of fried onions.) Only at weekends, when custom was brisk, did they work together. I had to grow accustomed to Daphne's brusque manner whenever I requested a fruit or vegetable that wasn't in stock: 'No,' she'd respond with a glower. 'Certainly not.' The milder-tempered Sis would reply to the effect that the desired item was too expensive at the moment or not to be found in the market.

I was walking in the park with Daphne one morning when

she revealed that the builders were working in, and redecorating, the large house above the shop. I asked, in all innocence, if she and Sis were having a new bathroom fitted. The very word 'bathroom' sent her into an immediate rage. 'Bathroom? Bathroom? We've never had a bathroom, and we're not getting one now. No, we're *not* having a bathroom fitted. I should think not.'

I had obviously caused offence, for she said nothing more, but fumed loudly instead. I, too, had grown up in a house without a bathroom, and remembered the complete bliss of taking a long, hot bath when I stayed with my mother's friends – the elderly couple who cared for me on those days my mother was working late.

We followed the dogs, who were happily sniffing every tree, before I ventured another question.

'Forgive my asking, Daphne, but where do you wash?'

'At the kitchen sink, of course.'

Of course. It was at the kitchen sink in Battersea that I washed and scrubbed myself to my mother's detailed instructions – 'Back as well as front,' she exhorted. We called it a 'strip wash' for you took off your clothing one piece at a time, washing each part of the body in turn, ending up with the feet, which you placed – one foot, then the other – in the now-scummy water. Of course.

'The kitchen sink was good enough for us when we were kids, and good enough for us today.' This was a fact, an unassailable fact, beyond argument, beyond logic.

'I love my bathroom.' I said. 'There's nothing better than a long soak when you're tired and aching.'

'I don't want no bathroom.' Her tone, at once both chastising and smug, hinted that I was decadent.

'Bathroom,' she muttered, contemptuously. 'Bathroom.'

I learned, in the park again, that the sisters shared a bed on the first floor. The upstairs rooms were seldom occupied, except on 'special occasions', the special nature of which Daphne did not disclose. They had been redecorated, 'just in case'.

It was Daphne's habit to stick a card in a cauliflower with the message NICE WITH A WHITE SAUCE. Rhubarb was similarly honoured: NICE IN A PIE WITH CUSTARD. Carrots were SAID TO BE GOOD FOR EYESIGHT, while AN APPLE A DAY KEEPS THE DOCTOR AWAY. Sis, who did most of the cooking, remarked to me whenever I bought Jersey potatoes, 'They're dirty little devils when they're cold.' I purchased Jerseys only from them in order to hear, and relish, this gnomic observation.

At the end of Sis's life, when her sight was fading, a neighbour drove the van to market. Trixie, or Tricksy, 'passed over' first. She had rarely seen a vet, for the sisters were as contemptuous of medics as they were of bathrooms. The limping, worn-out dog was distressing to look at, particularly when Circe – who was roughly the same age – was so lively. Daphne found herself another animal, who now follows her sluggishly around the park. Sis 'passed over' and Daphne closed down the business. She lives alone in that Victorian pile, still sleeping – I assume – in the bed she shared with Sis; still washing at the kitchen sink, and still covering a boiled cauliflower with a nice white sauce.

Poodles in Paradise

On a Saturday morning in December 1995, I was driven up to the town of Petrópolis, high in the hills above Rio. It was a typical Brazilian morning, I was told by the driver as I commented on the lush greenness all about us on the way – those sudden, dense showers followed by immediate warm sunshine ensured the healthy survival of plants, trees, flowers. You could call it the climate of Paradise, and that's what the poet Elizabeth Bishop did. Bishop, who was born in the less-than-paradisal Nova Scotia, lived in Brazil for ten, largely happy, years. She had a lover, the architect and designer Lota (full name Maria Carlota Costellat de Macedo) Soares, and she had two houses – one near São Paolo, and the other in Petrópolis. We were going to visit this second house, which she describes in 'Song for the Rainy Season':

> Hidden, oh hidden
> in the high fog
> the house we live in,
> beneath the magnetic rock,
> rain-, rainbow-ridden,
> where blood-black
> bromelias, lichens,
> owls, and the lint
> of the waterfalls cling,
> familiar, unbidden.

There was no fog that day, just the occasional rainy mist, but the magnetic rock was visible. Isabella, the young curator at the local Imperial Museum, met the six of us in the town square. For some years now, she disclosed, she had been in charge of taking research students and literary pilgrims, mostly American, to see the house. Its present owner, a rich woman with apartments in Paris and Rio, had been unaware that its previous occupant was a famous poet whose fame had increased since her death in 1979. Everything belonging or appertaining to Bishop had gone, we were soon to discover. It was the completeness of that expungement that both intrigued and saddened me.

Let me remember that glass-fronted house. There is only one sizeable room, divided by a walkway from the ground floor to the floor above. In 1995, it was furnished in execrable taste, and the sight of those vibrant, headache-inducing colours was the first shock. A glance at the bookshelves in the reception room confirmed that this was no longer Bishop's domain. Could the translator of *The Diary of 'Helena Morley'* have really found a use for Reader's Digest condensed books, and was she a secret connoisseur of Jack Higgins and the other avowedly populist authors beside him? I couldn't begin to imagine so, and it was then – prompted by my puzzled questioning – that Isabella revealed that the rich owner had cleared out everything that was left in the house when she purchased it in the 1970s. The furniture, the garish paintings, the uninviting *objets* were all hers.

The beautifully designed and ordered garden – Lota's work – was a bird sanctuary when the poet and the town planner lived together. As our tour progressed, we learned that the birds had flown. The only bird in view was a roguish parrot who was now confined to the house. He'd had a partner and offspring, but they had been set upon by a pack of poodles and slaughtered. Poodles? Murderous poodles? The lady of Paris and Rio bred them right here in Petrópolis. We would meet, and smell, them later.

There was, and probably still is, a hut halfway down the sloping garden. On opening the door, we discovered a bar – without bottles or glasses, but recognizably a bar. It was here that Elizabeth and Lota would sit in the evenings, in the midst of those now-vanished tropical birds. American poets and novelists who drink too much tend to favour the heavy stuff – bourbon, Scotch, vodka, tequila – unlike their European counterparts, who mostly favour wine or beer. Bishop enjoyed a cocktail, in which the potency of the liquor is temporarily disguised. When the motherly Lota was around, she drank moderately, but when her lover was away she put moderation behind her. Lota was often absent, due to her involvement in left-wing politics. Towards the end of Bishop's sojourn in Paradise, she was gone for weeks at a time, campaigning and electioneering. Whenever they were reunited, they had bitter, furious rows. Elizabeth returned to America. Lota followed her to New York and killed herself in a hotel.

Those 'facts', such as they are, tell only part of the story. Next to the house in Petrópolis is the chalet, designed for her by Lota, with its direct view of a waterfall, where Bishop worked – slowly, painstakingly – on her incomparable poetry. Her books and papers have been removed, but her spirit is present. There's a table and chair and the constant sound of water, and these are enough to summon her back. If there's a literary shrine to attract the devoted to Petrópolis, it's here, in this damp, restricted space, and nowhere else.

Just before we left, Madame's butler – in a white jacket, wearing white gloves – offered us glasses of fruit juice from a gleaming silver tray. It was then we were invited to inspect the kennels which had been specially built behind the house. It was here that Madame's poodles were bred. In December 1995, there were thirty-five of them, and the stench emanating from the kennels was not of the kind associated with an earthly Paradise.

I have never regarded the poodle as being properly canine. Like the chihuahua, its principal function appears to be as a fashion accessory. It seems to spend most of its charmed life in beauty parlours, where its coat is clipped and shampooed and from which it emerges looking ever more precious. A primped and cosseted poodle often comes to resemble its owner, and vice versa, especially when the fur on its head is bouffant, with dainty ribbons tied into bows over each ear. Madame's darlings may have murdered a parrot or two, but they looked appropriately snooty and pampered in Petrópolis that day. Luxury objects, in a luxurious setting.

I thought of Lota on the journey back to Rio – Lota, the radical who was one of the prevailing forces behind the creation of the park in the capital; Lota, who fought her lover's demons by giving her not one but two beautiful homes as well as the security of her trusting companionship. But Lota, who worked tirelessly to ease the plight of the poor, had her own demons – not least jealousy, and a sense of betrayal and loss. The way in which she brought her useful and dignified life to a close was cruel to Bishop but also cruel, lastingly cruel, to herself.

The poodle is privileged in Brazilian society, where the rich are very rich and the poor utterly destitute. Only about ten per cent of the huge population can read or write. God, for the children who live in shacks and caves, takes the form of the footballer who has escaped from the slums by dint of his natural talent, which has somehow been discovered early and nurtured. The statue of Christ the Redeemer – paid for by the French, sculpted by a Pole – so long the most imposing feature of Rio's skyline, looks down on a quotidian mélange of death and disorder. The young who die here daily are lucky if they can be identified – a mutilated corpse is just another mutilated corpse; one among thousands.

We were warned on arriving in Brazil to keep our watches and any jewellery we possessed in the hotel safe. There were nimble thieves in every street. One afternoon, attending a performance of the ballet *La Fille Mal Gardée* at the Opera House, I noticed several overdressed women nip into the Ladies relatively unadorned, only to reappear minutes later sporting bracelets, necklaces, earrings and – on one *grande dame* – a diamond tiara. Their chauffeurs had transported the jewels to the Opera House in locked metal boxes. The women wouldn't be seen dead in public without these tokens of their terrible wealth.

A society such as this has its quota of stray dogs, who exist on virtually the same level as those human beings who are themselves strays. Yet the poodle, bred by Madame's faithful staff in Petrópolis, is the breathing equivalent of the diamond brooch, the string of pearls. It does not look out of place next to a mink coat. It is, in every sense, a lapdog.

> I am his Highness' dog at Kew,
> Pray tell me, sir, whose dog are you?

Pope's lines came to me as I stared at those thirty-five prized treasures in the compound behind Elizabeth and Lota's portion of Paradise. I could imagine them saying much the same in Portuguese.

A close inspection of Christ the Redeemer reveals it to be kitsch, its potency as a symbol only powerful when seen from afar. The nearby tourist shops sell miniature Christs and tear-stained Virgin Marys alongside X-rated porno videos of 'highlights from the Carnival'. The participants in those stimulating 'highlights' are almost invariably men – men who look like men, and men disguised as, or surgically transformed into, women; the brightly plumed transvestites and transsexuals who strut each night in Copacabana. The shack- or cave-dwelling boy who thinks he should have been born a girl has a chance of survival in this decadent culture, particularly if he is prettier than his sister. He could become a rich man's plaything, with luck. If he can escape being raped or murdered, he will be wearing jewels and furs and the finest silk lingerie by the time he is in his twenties. He will have a woman's name by then, and a certain kind of woman's aspirations, which might include the ownership of a poodle from Petrópolis.

Summer Snows

Grief melts away
Like snow in May,
As if there were no such cold thing

writes George Herbert in 'The Flower', the most affecting poem of renewal and hopefulness in English. And Herbert, bless his sweet and inquisitive nature, is right, for grief does have a habit of evaporating – suddenly, without warning, inexplicably.

I was in Florence two summers after David's death. I had visited the Brancacci Chapel at eleven and eaten lunch at Angiolino's, the *trattoria* I had frequented in the late 1960s. (One of the waiters from that time was still serving – a melancholy looking man who bore a close resemblance to the lugubrious French comic actor Fernandel. He was older, greyer, and his expression was more hangdog than ever.) I climbed, that warm but not overpoweringly hot afternoon, the several steep roads that lead to Forte Belvedere, which affords – as its name suggests – a wonderful view of the city. It was while I was looking down on the pink and green splendours of the Duomo and the Campanile that I found myself happily weeping. I was glad, overwhelmingly glad, to be alive and in possession of such beauty. These were the first contented tears I had shed since that March morning when I kissed his cold, untroubled forehead as he lay at peace at last.

And then, in 1992, in Trieste, something similar happened. It was a warm day and again I had eaten lunch – a simple meal of grilled sole and salad – but on this occasion I was looking at water, at the huge ferry boats waiting to go to Brindisi and Corfu. Jane was in my mind now as I recalled the letter she sent me following our delightful eating tour of Scotland. From Glasgow, where we said our goodbyes, she had driven down to the Lake District. It was there, by Lake Windermere, that she discovered she wanted to live for the first time since November 1985, the month Geoffrey died. But it was too late, for the cancer she was battling against was advanced to a stage beyond cure.

It was with this bittersweet memory of her that I once more felt the joy of simply existing, of being in the city of Svevo and Saba, two much-loved writers. And I remembered that Geoffrey had hated the idea of extinction and often quoted those lines by Herbert

>And now in age I bud again,
>After so many deaths I live and write

Which is what I am doing, even as I know that melted grief can ice over in the night or in the dense darkness of early morning, before daylight brings some hope of continuance.

Dude

He was wearing the most flamboyant of all his flamboyant outfits a few days before he was murdered in December 2000. This was his masterpiece, no doubt of it, and unlikely to be eclipsed. A thin, lithe black man, who always walked with a spring in his step – he sometimes seemed to be bouncing along the road – was dressed in a grey suit. But this was no ordinary grey suit. This was a grey suit with a familiar story to tell. As he came towards me, I saw the smiling Marilyn Monroe of the Andy Warhol collage. Her hair, her eyes, her teeth, all glowing, were there on his jacket and trousers – each part of her face concertinaed with the movement of his arms and legs.

The black-and-white photography was now a uniform grey. He had chosen a lace-frilled black shirt and a floppy black silk handkerchief to offset the prevailing greyness. He had no wish, ever, to appear drab. Grey and black were colours, and on him they looked colourful. They certainly seemed so on that mild winter morning. He was striding to the market as usual, in search of the fabrics with the outré designs he had made his own. What would he find to replace Marilyn, his *pièce de résistance*? (It was, as far as I, his silent admirer, was concerned.) Whatever he found, it was not to be transformed – lovingly tailored by his sister, I learned later – into one of his incomparable suits.

He came across as a man of means – albeit modest, for the materials available in Shepherd's Bush market are not those favoured by the master tailors of Savile Row. He nevertheless behaved like a devotee of *haute couture*, because he never wore the same suit twice. (His sister must have spent the greater part of each working day toiling at her sewing machine.) But what were his means? How could he afford to live a life of such obvious leisure?

It would be easy to describe him as a dandy, but the word smacks too much of the elegant and the stylish. The dandy is invariably well dressed, and often quietly so, the distinction of his garments unobtrusive, like the prose of the great classic authors. You couldn't help noticing the young man's shirts, in a variety of garish shades; his natty bowlers and fedoras; his two-toned shoes; his umbrellas and canes. He was parodying the elegance of the rich as best he could, and his best was frequently considerable. He caused me to gawp, and he made me smile.

No, the word for him is 'dude'. He reminded me of James Cagney, swaggering cockily whether as winner or loser in the gangster movies of the 1930s: of George Raft in the middle sequence of *Scarface*; of Marlon Brando as Sky Masterson in *Guys and Dolls*. Like them, he had a touch of the tawdry, and gave off more than a passing hint that he probably wasn't on the right side of the law.

His killer, or killers, contrived to make his death look like suicide. The police had to cut him down. The reason, the cold reason, for his death was drugs.

Circe barked at him once – out of appreciation, perhaps. He paid her no attention. He paid nobody attention on his daily walks among us. His mind must have been pleasantly occupied with something or other, for he was never gloomy or sad. He was happy in his body, I reckoned, and that's as much happiness as anyone wants, or can expect.

The Last Morning Walk

When she was about ten years old, Circe's front paws started to grow larger. The vet, Michael Gordon, diagnosed arthritis, and set her on a course of antibiotics. He warned me that if the disease spread, her legs would give way and she would have to be put down. He spoke, as ever, with genuine concern and a certain sadness that such a vigorous life should be brought to an end in this cruel fashion.

But the arthritis didn't spread, and the pills did their beneficent work. The paws stayed the same, causing children to remark on her big feet. Her energy was unabated. She ran as she'd always run, defying exhaustion until it claimed her. Exhaustion came sooner now, but not *that* soon.

Then, in her fifteenth year, Circe's bladder became uncontrollable. She looked at us guiltily as urine flowed from her. She had been fastidious about the necessary functions even before puppyhood was over, dragging her walker to the kerb whenever she felt the need to vacate her insides. She never fouled the pavement. But now that she was helpless, her sad brown eyes made her loss of dignity apparent.

Once again, Michael Gordon recommended a magic cure, in the form of a syrup that tightened her sphincter. She stopped peeing in the house, and woke us in the middle of the night by scratching at the door to indicate that she wanted to go out as quickly as possible. Her self-esteem was restored. We lived with this considerate routine of Circe's devising for several months.

She grew increasingly deaf, she who had once been able to bark at the presence of another dog two streets away. The syrup lost its magical properties, and the guilty looks multiplied. She was entering an undignified old age.

Jeremy and I decided that it was in Circe's interests, rather than our own, that her life should, at last, be ended. I phoned Michael Gordon's surgery and made an appointment to take her in when he was on duty. I couldn't bear the thought of a stranger, however kindly and experienced, injecting her with the drugs that would ease her out of the world. The terrible deed was almost done.

We rose early that summer morning in 2001. It was going to be a bright, sunny day. A final run in Ravenscourt Park seemed the pleasantest, tenderest way of saying goodbye to her.

It was with dismay that we found that the park was closed – had been cordoned off, in fact. The adjacent streets were jammed with police cars. It appeared that a small girl had gone missing, and the park was being combed for any clues to her whereabouts.

There is a pocket-sized strip of green in an apology for a park only yards from the house. That's where we threw the ball for her to retrieve with something of her former speed and dexterity. Although our intentions were humane, we felt like murderers as she ran backwards and forwards in all innocence. Jeremy consulted his watch. It was time to be off.

I stroked Circe's head and ears while Jeremy drove us to the vet. Michael Gordon was waiting for us. Circe wagged her tail as he said hello to her. She was given her first injection, and then he carried her to a nearby room, where he laid her on a table. We sat beside her, stroking her in turns until her eyes closed on us. She received a second, fatal, dose and we went on sitting beside her, unable to control our tears.

We left her eventually. Jeremy set off for work, and I walked home, oblivious to the sunshine. She'd had a charmed life, I assured myself, and a happy one. I remembered my own good fortune on the day David sent me to buy a new sieve and I acquired a puppy as well. A foolish, madcap, impractical decision it seemed at the time. But now I fully understood that it had been a wise one, and a blessing.

Coda

On 22 September 2002, I spent a wonderful day on a boat in the Danube Delta. This is Romania's most substantial beauty spot, and the sun blazed down on it. Wildlife thrives there, though all I saw as I chatted with British and Romanian friends was the occasional flock of – to me – unidentifiable birds. The wildest inhabitants come out at night, when the boats are safely moored.

Late in the evening, I went for a last drink to the country retreat owned by the Writers' Union in Neptun, a town on the Black Sea. I had noticed, on previous visits, a pack of stray dogs in the gardens. The writers threw them scraps, which they instantly devoured. I learned that, in late October, when the retreat closed for the winter months, the animals – there were cats, too – would be left to fend for themselves, with no one to give them the odd pieces of chicken or fish or steak they had enjoyed in the spring and summer.

A black-and-white mongrel puppy, with impossibly long floppy ears, came to where I was sitting. Oh God, I thought, I'm back in the market, gazing dementedly at an entrancing creature. I stroked her black coat and white belly and admired the white spots above each eye. I decided that I would try to rescue her and bring her home, somehow, to England.

At three a.m. on the morning of 23 September, I awoke from an uneasy sleep, gasping for breath. At eight I was in the local hospital, having an ECG and wearing an oxygen mask.

A woman doctor informed me that I had suffered heart failure and that I would be transferred to the big hospital in Constanța for tests. I could not fly without the assistance and company of a qualified nurse or doctor.

I passed a single night in the Intensive Care ward. I peed constantly into cut-off Fanta or Coca-Cola bottles, listening to the screams of a man with skin like alabaster dying in the next bed. The nurse on duty, Valentina, gave me a sedative, and when I came to some hours later, the screams had abated, and three women – his wife and daughters – had lit candles over his body, lighting him, Orthodox fashion, to a better world.

I returned to London, where I was treated with great care and skill at Hammersmith Hospital. A Romanian doctor in the Cardiology Unit translated the copious notes, accurate in every detail, that her counterpart in Constanța had written.

I hope the puppy is being cared for, but I doubt it. If only I had seen her earlier. If only I'd had the strength to go through with the whole complicated business of rescuing her. I would have called her Dido.